The Spanish-American Independence Movement

Simón Bolívar. Credit: New York Public Library Picture Collection.

The Spanish-American Independence Movement

JAY KINSBRUNER
Queens College

The Dryden Press
901 North Elm Street
Hinsdale, Illinois 60521

Library of Congress Catalog Card Number: 72-95711
ISBN: 03-085190-4
Printed in the United States of America
345-065-987654321

For Mac Kinsbruner

Preface

The Spanish American independence movement, for all its eventfulness, has only just begun to win the attention of a wide audience in this country. The present book is intended for this audience, members of which manifest understandably different interests and tastes. My central goal has been to guide the reader through a complicated period of Spanish American history and help him see the problems of emergent nationhood in what I consider their proper historical perspective. To this end I have concentrated on those aspects of society, and on those problems which provide this perspective. I have not attempted to present the kind of "balanced account" that one might find in an elementary text. Indeed, my focus is on, to use a term popular in the early nineteenth century, the *active citizenry*—the oligarchy in the colonial period and the oligarchy and those citizens on the way up from the lower ranks of society in the national period. Spanish Americans included in the active citizenry anyone with the right to vote, but this renders the term meaningless. Many people during the early national period had the right to vote but played a passive role in society; they are therefore not included in my definition of the active citizenry. This active citizenry carried out the independence movement and to a considerable degree determined the character of the new nations.

Probably it would be salutary if someone would write a book about the Spanish American independence movement without ever mentioning the great liberators—men like Bolívar, San Martín, O'Higgins, Hidalgo, and Morelos. We have been so overwhelmed by their presence and deeds that we have often failed to discern visible clues to the nature of the emergent societies and states, clues that help us understand the successes and failures of the early national period. Since this book is intended for a mixed audience, I have felt it necessary to mention these dominant figures, but I have tried to keep their biographies and the discussion of their military deeds to a minimum.

The term *Spanish American* appears in the title of this book rather than *Latin American* because the book does not deal with Brazil. The experiences of the Portuguese empire and Brazil are different enough to warrant separate treatment.

In a book of this sort one incurs many debts. My greatest debt obviously has been to the many historians whose works I have used in developing my ideas and in writing the volume. I have tried to give some indication of the extent of this debt in the bibliography. Professor Ralph della Cava read the manuscript and offered many suggestions. My conversations with him over the years have had a profound effect on the genesis of the present book. I should like to thank also Professor Keith Eubank for reading the manuscript and making many perceptive suggestions. Professor John E. Fagg read and improved the Wheelwright sections in an earlier version. Professor Marvin D. Bernstein and Professor Arnold J. Bauer both read parts of the book in an earlier version and made valuable comments. Professor Margaret E. Crahan was kind enough to answer questions relating to the colonial period. I thank all these colleagues, but naturally I am the only one responsible for the errors in fact or judgment which may appear in the book. Without the ceaseless efforts of the staff of the Queens College library, especially

Professor Solena Bryant and Mr. Leonard Cohen, this book could hardly have been undertaken. Mrs. Lila Hillman and Mr. Herbert Sakofsky assisted in the preparation of the manuscript for publication. Finally, I should like to thank my wife, Karen, for taking time from her own professional duties to proofread and edit the manuscript on several occasions.

Contents

Maps

CHAPTER ONE

Introduction

The purpose of this introductory chapter is to highlight several fundamental characteristics of Spanish America's colonial heritage that have not always received their due attention. These characteristics play a vital part in the development of the central themes presented in this book. An awareness of them is essential for an understanding of the nature of the Spanish American independence movement and the problems faced by the emergent nations.

The Spains

At the time of the fall of the last Moorish stronghold of Granada and the discovery of America in 1492 Spain was only apparently a united monarchy. In substance

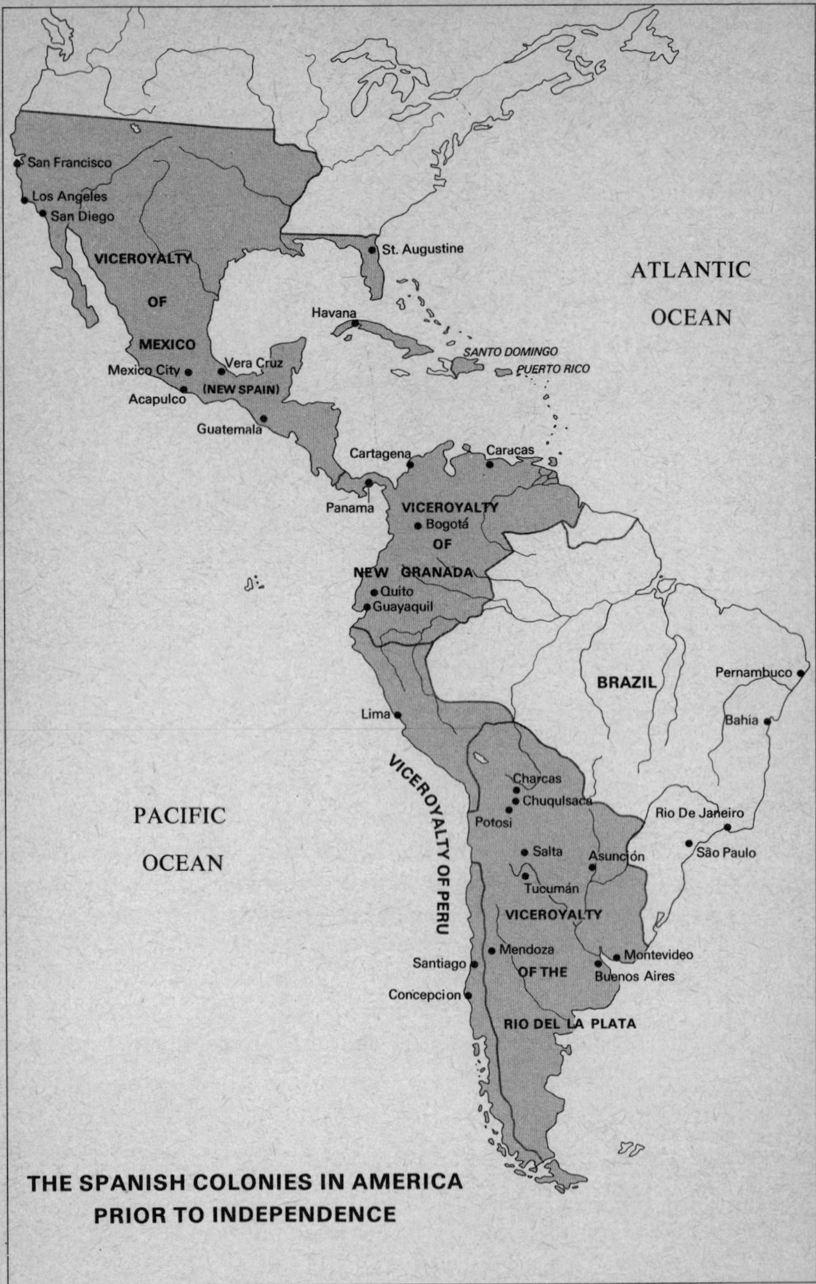

THE SPANISH COLONIES IN AMERICA PRIOR TO INDEPENDENCE

SPANISH AMERICA AT THE END OF THE WARS OF INDEPENDENCE

there actually existed a federation of principalities joined together in a personal union through the marriage of Ferdinand and Isabel. There were two main administrative units: Ferdinand's Aragon and Isabel's Castile. With the incorporation of Granada into the crown of Castile in 1492 Isabel's patrimony comprised about two-thirds of the area of the entire Iberian peninsula. It overwhelmed Ferdinand's Aragon in both size and population, and at the time of the conquest and colonization of America it had the more dynamic economy.

Over the centuries Aragon and Castile had developed quite differently. The kingdom of Aragon, following the lead of one of its states, Catalonia, assumed decidedly commercial and imperial characteristics during the thirteenth and fourteenth centuries. Catalan merchants ranged through the entire Mediterranean world, winning markets for their iron and textiles and in the process contributing to the establishment of a formal empire. Thus Sardinia and Sicily became part of the crown of Aragon in 1409. During these centuries the most powerful sector in the Aragonese society was the urban bourgeoisie, the commercial-capitalist class. Aragon's territorial nobility, except in rare instances, was not as impressive as its Castilian counterpart and, while trade was flourishing, not a match for the commercial sector.

Sometimes in harmony and sometimes in conflict with the crown, this trading society worked out a constitutional system palpably unlike the one developing in Castile. This society was fervently dedicated to the concept of contractual government. Through the various parliaments, the *Cortes*, the Aragonese institutionalized the concept that a contract of mutual trust existed between the king and his subjects. Each had contractually limited powers and privileges. The extent of this contractualism is tellingly demonstrated in the oath of allegiance to the king: "We who are so good as you swear to you who are no better than we, to accept you as our king and sovereign lord, provided you observe all our liberties and laws; but if not, not."[1]

At the time of independence the Spanish Americans did not have to search out foreign intellectuals for the concepts of contractual government and limited monarchy. They were very much a part of Spanish political tradition.

Castile developed differently. By 1492 the landed aristocracy had established itself firmly and was clearly the leading economic force in the kingdom. Unlike the crown of Aragon, where the urban bourgeoisie became the vigor of the economy and the ascendant class, in Castile the landed aristocracy, with the feudal nobility at its head, dominated the economy, society, and politics. To forge a central and absolutist monarchy in Castile Ferdinand and Isabel had to destroy the entrenched power of this aristocracy and nobility.

This is not to suggest that an urban bourgeoisie did not exist in Castile, for in fact one did exist. Merchants in Castile were not only powerful but were also involved in extensive foreign trade. In part because of their romantic attractiveness too much attention has been focused on the landed aristocracy, and often there has been a failure to recognize the intense urbanization taking place in Castile and the vitality of its urban bourgeoisie.

In their concerted efforts to break the power of the landed aristocracy and the feudal nobility Ferdinand and Isabel relied heavily on the urban bourgeoisie and supported its development both directly and indirectly. For instance, towns were given many privileges that directly contradicted the feudal regime. By 1492 the Catholic kings had effectively broken the political power of the feudal nobility. Yet at the time of the fall of Granada and the discovery of America the feudal nobility and landed aristocracy continued to enjoy their traditional social and economic position. Thus while there was an impressive urban growth and a significant urban-based bourgeoisie in Castile by 1492, the society continued to be lorded over by the landed aristocracy (including those nobles who were able to survive and compete after the reduction of their political powers), and the economy continued to be presided over mainly by the landed interests.

Spain and America

Columbus discovered America for Isabel, not for Spain or the Spanish people. Therefore the colonies belonged to the crown of Castile and not to Spain, something that had grave consequences for the Spanish empire in 1808. The Spanish American colonies took on the characteristics of Castile rather more than Aragon. The early nobility, the system of large landed estates, the landed aristocracy, the imperial government established in Castile, the system of trade controlled and serviced by Castilians, and the crown's attempts, notably after the early 1540s, to transfer Castile's brand of royal absolutism to the New World all serve to remind one how much Castile influenced the empire's developing personality.

Yet it is sometimes overlooked how very much Castile was not a monolithic society, how many tens of thousands of people resided in towns, how strong the urban bourgeoisie actually was (though overshadowed socially and economically by the landed rich), and how very much Spaniards other than Castilians contributed to the maturing colonial character over the centuries. People from all over Spain settled in the colonies during the four centuries of empire; and they brought with them their regional characteristics, some of which were antithetical to the presence of a feudal nobility, an exclusive landed aristocracy, and even royal absolutism.

In 1492 Spain and the colonies were centrally capitalist and not feudal, although there were distinct feudal overtones. The considerable emphasis on urbanization, the presence in many places of a large and powerful urban-based commercial class—a bourgeoisie—and especially in Aragon a manifest predilection toward contractual government and limited monarchy were Spanish characteristics that were also transferred to the colonies, along with the system of large estates and the legendary landed aristocracy.

The Formal Institutions of Colonization

While highlighting several especially important features of Spanish America's colonial heritage it would be worthwhile to examine briefly the formal institutions of colonization.

The Council of the Indies, officially established in 1542, was the dominant imperial organ during the first two centuries of empire. It was the crown's chief advisory body, it drafted legislation pertaining to the American empire, and it was the appellate judicial court for all significant civil cases originating in the colonies. From 1717 the council was reduced to a judicial body, and its impressive administrative and legislative functions were invested in a new Ministry of the Marine and the Indies. The second most important and powerful governing institution was the famous House of Trade, established in Seville in 1503 and moved to Cádiz in 1717-18. It administered the mercantile system and thus controlled trade in all its ramifications.

At the head of each colonial government stood the viceroy—the vice-king—who was the direct representative of the crown, charged with supervising the entire colonial administration. He had to execute legislation, insure order and stability, hold frontier regions, and, often most importantly, produce revenue for the royal coffers. The viceroy had his own advisory body, known as the *audiencia*, which also was the leading judicial agency in the viceroyalties. As an appellate court it ranked directly below the Council of the Indies. But in addition to advising the viceroy, the *audiencia* had its own legislative privileges. Such were the range and effectiveness of the *audiencia's* powers that the viceroys were sometimes constrained to the point of virtual impotence. A strong *audiencia* could neutralize a weak viceroy and in effect supersede him in the colonial hierarchy.

Audiencias varied in size and power, and each viceroyalty was made up of many of them. The *audiencias* located in the viceregal capitals and presided over by the viceroy himself were traditionally the most powerful in the viceroyalty. During the first two centuries of empire there were only two viceroyalties—those of New Spain (Mexico), established in 1535, and Peru, established in 1542. The viceroyalty of New Granada was created in 1717, and the viceroyalty of the Río de la Plata (Argentina) was created in 1776. The viceroyalties sometimes had jurisdiction over smaller administrative units called captaincies general.

Beneath the viceroys and captains general were the provincial governors. And finally at the bottom of the pyramidal hierarchy of the colonial institutions were the town councils, the *cabildos* or *ayuntamientos*. It was crown policy to appoint Spaniards born in Spain (known as peninsulars) to the leading colonial posts but not to exclude Spaniards born in America (called *criollos* or creoles) from the lesser positions, especially in the town councils. Thus it turned out that the *cabildos* became the most obvious institution of creole political power and influence.

What Spain established in America, then, was a system of regional government, and this not unnaturally contributed to a robust spirit of regionalism during the national period.

One final institution of colonization, the Catholic church, the colonizing agent par excellence, deserves much of the credit for the establishment, stability, and permanence of the empire. The church was enormously powerful in the colonies. Individual clergymen could easily undermine loyalty and civil obedience from the pulpit, by their general contact with the natives, or through their own example. But the church had far more subtle ways of influencing the population.

In many areas the entire economy revolved around the economic activities of the church. Often the best estates, the most efficient and profitable haciendas, were owned and operated by the regular orders. Even greater influence was secured through the church's banking operations. The church loaned money to the lay public at the standard 5 percent interest. The involvement of such capital in the colonial economy is truly staggering. Just at the end of the colonial period the bishop-elect of Michoacán, Abad y Queipo, estimated that of the two hundred thousand people engaged in economic activities in Mexico, not a hundred operated fully with their own personal capital. The majority were deeply in debt to the church. With so much of the economy of Mexico and other colonies critically dependent on the church for its basic capital, it is clear that the church was in an enviable position to influence its flock, a good many of whom would have been ruined had their loans been called in or had new capital been made unavailable.

The Empire's Economic Rationale

The first and foremost fact about Spain's colonial economy is that the colonies existed for the benefit of the mother country. The economic system which governed the relations between Spain and the colonies was mercantilism. Although the state involved itself in all aspects of the economy, mercantilism was essentially a capitalist system. Clearly it was not laissez faire capitalism; but it was based on the profit motive, it was a commercial system, and it involved production for the external (colonial) market. It even emphasized nonagricultural production, at least in theory, since Spain was never properly suited to its own mercantilist concepts. Without a strong manufacturing section it actually became a middleman for European goods being shipped to the colonies and for the colonial bullion that consequently had to be transshipped to the rest of Europe.

The mercantile system was governed by the House of Trade, which enforced and often created the minute and encompassing regulations that served the mercantilist rationale. In the colonies it was aided by the merchant tribunals, the *consulados*. Together they supervised the *flota* system, a procedure whereby commercial ships would travel to and from the colonies in regularly scheduled fleets under the protection of the royal navy. There were usually two annual fleet sailings, each comprising fifty or more ships. One was destined for Veracruz and the other for Panama and Cartagena. The ships would meet at Havana for the return trip the following year. This meant that the basic trade between Spain and the colonies was carried out under tight supervision and to the decided advantage of the Seville and Cádiz merchants. They and the members of the colonial *consulados* enjoyed clear benefits from this de facto monopolistic system.

What the crown established was in no uncertain terms a colonial system in which the periphery existed for the benefit of the metropolis, although not as effectively as the crown desired. The irony is that Spain's inherent weakness as a mercantile power meant that over the course of the colonial centuries the metropolis turned out to be not Madrid but a series of other European capitals.

Feudalism, Capitalism, and the Colonial Bourgeoisie

For generations it has been popular to say that Spanish American society was feudal or semifeudal and that it has been dominated by a retroactive "oligarchic triarchy" or "tripartite aristocracy." This controlling triarchy is supposed to have included the upper clergy, the army officers, and the landed aristocracy. The tripartite theory has little tolerance for the presence of a commercial class–no less a dynamic one that has shared political power with other leading elements in society–and does much to obscure our understanding of Spanish American social history.

In fact, it would be more proper to state that the Spanish American society and economy have been centrally capitalist with some notable feudal overtones. And while there has been a good deal of social stratification, with the landholding aristocracy maintaining an ascendant position, the society has included a commercial class–a bourgeoisie–that has shared political, social, and economic power with the landed rich. The relationship of the landed aristocracy to Spanish America's quest for development and progress is quite well known and understood, although one need not overlook the many landed rich who were concerned with progress and equity. Just as well known is the relationship of the dependent classes–the Indians and mixed-bloods–who have comprised the vast majority of the population, to Spanish America's chronic underdevelopment. What is not generally appreciated is the degree to which the colonial bourgeoisie has contributed to the character of the emergent nations and consequently to the progress or retardation, the stability or instability, the development or underdevelopment that followed independence. Before examining the colonial bourgeoisie more closely it is necessary to put the concepts of feudalism and capitalism in their proper perspective.

Feudalism

Essentially the Spanish American colonial economy was not feudal. There were large landed estates in Spanish America, but these were not generally dedicated to self-sufficient agrarian production or production for the needs of the immediate environment. Rather the landed estates were designed for production for distant markets; they were export oriented. In the early colonial period the landed rich might not have been as profit oriented as were the merchants, but as the merchants grew in numbers and power the landowners had to produce profit in order to compete with them for social, political, and economic status.

Yet there were feudal overtones. The most significant was the *encomienda*, a grant of Indian labor. This has been taken by many to have been quite essentially feudal in nature; however, as with the landed estates, this was not designed for a limited or self-sufficient agrarian and artisan production but rather for the exportation of precious metals and crops. The *encomendero* was an entrepreneur very much tied to the world capitalist market. Whether the system was feudal or slave for the Indian is almost irrelevant; it was intolerable either way.

But there was a very prominent feudal remnant in the colonial economy. Forms of serfdom existed in the colonial period and long thereafter. Those peasant farmers who were lucky enough to get their own land to work very often did so by making a deal with the large landowners whereby the peasant was given a piece of land in return for labor-services on the owner's estate. Serfdom was not limited strictly to the feudal period. Engels understood this: "It is certain that serfdom and villeinage are not a specifically medieval-feudal form, it occurs everywhere or almost everywhere, where conquerors have made the native inhabitants cultivate the soil for them."[2] E. J. E. Hobsbawm, the noted British Marxist economist, has demonstrated that a form of feudal serfdom is even extant in contemporary Spanish America. Hobsbawm has shown that feudal institutions can be reproduced in a contemporary capitalist environment. Studying the province of La Convención, Peru, he has demonstrated that peasants were so burdened by a system of neofeudal labor-services in payment for land usage they were not able to cultivate their own land as efficiently as they would have liked. Some tenants received plots as large as twenty to twenty-five hectares (about fifty acres), although because of the labor-service requirements they generally exploited only four to six hectares. There is even evidence to indicate that tenant holdings were more efficient than the haciendas and that the former produced a greater percentage of their crops for the external market than did the latter, which is to say that the tenants were relatively highly commercialized and quite involved in the world capitalist system. Under a more genuinely capitalist economic arrangement, such as sharecropping without labor-service requirements, there is reason to believe that tenants would have cultivated far more land than they did and that consequently their production would have increased markedly. Thus here we have a definite case of feudal obligations limiting agricultural development in an underdeveloped country.

The presence of imposing numbers of neofeudal tenant farmers in a fundamentally capitalist system limited the full maturing of capitalism and impeded the successful transition from preindustrial to industrial capitalism. This theme shall be explored further in the following section.

A final point about feudalism is that its political structure was never established in Spanish America. There was something approaching a feudal nobility during the early decades after the discovery and especially after the conquest of Mexico, but the crown soon took pains to prevent the genuine creation of such a nobility, and determined in fact to guarantee the presence of royal absolutism. By the end of the colonial period many of the titles of Castile were held by merchants or merchant-landowners, men who were hardly feudal nobles.

Capitalism

By any of the several accepted definitions of capitalism it is clear that the Spanish American colonial economy was fundamentally capitalist and not feudal. One definition in particular–Marx's definition–illumines the problems faced by the emergent nations. Marx considered the coalescence of several phenomena as necessary for the full emergence of capitalism out of feudalism. Spanish America lacked two especially prominent ones at the end of the colonial period and during the early national period, to say nothing of the late nineteenth and early twentieth centuries. One of them was the general absence throughout Spanish America of highly developed strong urban craft guilds, those medieval institutions which helped so much in raising labor to the level of property, that is, to the level of a commodity. There were indeed craft guilds, but in the vast majority of cases these never reached the high degree of development associated with the European guilds. The quality of their products was generally inferior, and they never attained the local political status of the major craft guilds in Europe. True, their powers therefore did not have to be overcome as a prerequisite for the transition to industrial capitalism, but neither did Spanish America enjoy the benefits of a strong urban craft guild development. European guilds not only contributed to the creation of a standard of business ethics in their communities, they were often sources of the "original accumulation" so necessary for the development of capitalism and finally industrialization.

The absence of such a craft guild system in Spanish America appears to have been one of the internal factors which limited the colonies' potential for structural development as they became independent and moved into the industrial nineteenth century.

The presence of a proletariat is another development that is not only necessary for the rise of capitalism but that contributes to the successful transition from preindustrial to industrial capitalism. During both the eighteenth and nineteenth centuries there was a class of small farmers who, through any or several of a whole catalog of arrangements, managed to possess the land which they worked. These arrangements served to permit hundreds of thousands of small farmers to exist (and often little else) on the land. They mitigated against the establishment of a true proletariat of free, contractual workers, some of whom would have remained in the rural regions and others of whom would have left the land for the urban centers. The absence of a class of true proletarians impedes the development of capitalism. Under the conditions of their employment, so to speak, the rural masses neither added sufficiently to the demand of the internal market nor presented themselves as an industrial proletariat to accelerate the industrial process (and during the process perhaps become radicalized). There were groups of landless peasants, but until nearly the end of the nineteenth century there were always sufficient safety-valve features, such as the availability of cheap food and the possibility of emigration, to prevent the establishment of a permanent, stationary proletariat subject to radicalization. There were also large groups of urban workers who were tied to their jobs and employers through a series of neofeudal arrangements and who consequently did not become modern proletarians during the early nineteenth century.

Thus to understand the problems confronting the newly independent Spanish American countries one should take into consideration certain internal factors, such as the immature craft guild development, the presence of a large class of neofeudal small farmers, and the absence of a modern proletariat.

The Colonial Bourgeoisie

There was a dynamic bourgeoisie in Spain at the time of the discovery of America, and representatives of it settled in the new colonies. This they continued to do throughout the colonial period. The Spanish American colonies developed their own bourgeoisie, comprised not only of merchants and miners but, it could be argued, even some agrarians. By the end of the eighteenth century there was a strong and dynamic bourgeoisie in Spanish America. In 1673 a viceroy of Mexico observed: "It can be generally reckoned that for the most part in these provinces the gentleman is a merchant and the merchant is a gentleman." Another viceroy believed that everyone in Spanish America wanted to be rich "and to be so, all want to be merchants."[3]

The existence of this bourgeoisie belies the traditional description of a "colonial siesta." Relatively speaking, there may have been one during the first centuries, especially during the seventeenth century depression, but this was certainly not the case during the eighteenth. In the eighteenth century Spanish American merchants were involved in all sorts of commercial ventures, from the simple to the most complicated and even brilliant. Some of their schemes involved great sums of money and the use of agents in several countries.

By the end of the colonial period the merchants and miners enjoyed considerable political power at the local level of government. For instance, in the capital of the south of Chile, Concepción, 65 percent of all the town attorneys were merchants between 1790 and 1810. And during the same period, 55 percent of the more powerful of the two *alcaldes* (there were two categories of *alcaldes*, judges with mayoral functions) were merchants. In the important mining capital of Guanajuato, Mexico, every significant merchant and mining establishment was represented on the town council in 1778. And many more of these merchants were creoles than is generally thought. A famous example of the power of the merchants is that of Juan Martínez de Rozas, the most important political figure in the south of Chile in 1810. Rozas, a creole, was married to the daughter of the south's richest merchant. This marriage made him son-in-law, brother-in-law, and nephew-in-law to probably the leading merchants in the south. For a while after the independence movement commenced Rozas controlled the government of Chile.

Not only was there an important bourgeoisie in Spanish America by the end of the colonial period, one that had achieved great economic prosperity and enjoyed impressive political power, but it was a class very much like the other bourgeoisies of the western world. These western bourgeoisies gave us contractual government in the modern period, the concept of limited monarchy, and Locke's liberalism. The bourgeois way of life demanded stable governments, the rule of law, technological innovation, and an open society. By open society the bourgeoisie conceived of a society not stratified into estates. Though it was still a society of classes, the classes were fundamentally economic, lines were not strictly drawn, and one could, through his own efforts, move from one class to another. This is not to suggest that members of the upper classes were not jealous and protective of their position or that those of the lower were not unaware of the fact that they were clearly not in the upper classes and that the gulf which separated them—and which isolated them from obvious special privileges—was terribly difficult to overcome.

Though it represented a very small percentage of the entire population, the bourgeoisie formed the core of the active citizenry of the new Spanish American nations. In those places where the active citizenry had taken on the characteristics of a bourgeoisie one could find, to one degree or another, the social institutionalization of the profit motive as a way of life, a decided predilection for Lockean classical liberalism, a clear interest in and dependence on technological improvements, and the obvious presence of an open society in which an individual's drive and talents could get him all the way up or down the economic ladder and could determine his place in the active citizenry.

The Static Society

It is true that late colonial Spanish American society was quite static, but past emphasis on its feudal nature has contributed to an underestimation of the extraordinary degree to which the society was dynamic and even, in places, in a state of flux. Contributing to this society, which was less static than the traditional picture would suggest, was the presence of the bourgeoisie, a marked urbanization, many frontier regions, and often a high rate of population growth.

Many colonial urban centers held populations of tens of thousands of people. Even in provincial regions there was a good deal of urbanization. For instance, in the south of Chile during the final decades of the colonial period there were ten towns with larger populations than the capital of the south, Concepción. And at that time Concepción had a population of nearly five thousand people! There are presently too few demographic studies to allow an accurate generalization concerning the actual degree of urbanization in Spanish America at the end of the colonial period. But when we begin to speak of urban agglomerations of more than four or five thousand inhabitants it would be unsafe to conclude that they did not contribute to social fluidity and to the rise of bourgeoisies that would be more or less recognizable in the mainstream of Western bourgeois development. Probably Spanish America on the eve of independence was far more urban than is generally believed.

Spanish America was famous for its frontier regions. These generally did not support stable or static societies; rather they contributed to somewhat instable and dynamic societies. And in some places a high rate of population growth doubtless generated social instability rather than stability.

Colonial Spanish American society was probably ready for a revolution in 1810. What it got, however, was only a change in government.

Notes

1. Quoted in J. H. Elliot, *Imperial Spain, 1469-1716* (New York, 1966), p. 3.

2. Quoted in E. J. E. Hobsbawm's introduction to Karl Marx, *Pre-Capitalist Economic Formations* (New York, 1966), p. 59.

3. Quoted in David Brading, *Miners and Merchants in Bourbon Mexico, 1763-1810* (Cambridge, 1971), pp. 21 and 95.

CHAPTER TWO

The Causes of Independence

Independence movements seem to have a forceful attraction and the Spanish American movement is no exception. A knowledge of why an independence movement occurs is valuable if it permits a better understanding of the character of the new nation. But important clues are often pushed aside by the weight of interminable academic debate. The Spanish American independence movement has been mired in such debate in part for a very good reason: We seem determined to find the causes of an event that was a by product of the Napoleonic seizure of the Spanish throne in 1808. The Spanish American independence movement clearly was not the result of the momentum of a series of internal causes. On the other hand, aspects of the colonial system did in fact contrive to make independence palatable and even desirable once the Spanish Americans developed a taste for governing themselves in the name of the deposed King Ferdinand VII.

When Ferdinand was restored to the throne and proclaimed the reestablishment of royal absolutism in 1814, many of the colonies decided on true independence. But this decision must be viewed in the context of several years of actual self-government and the enjoyment of a whole array of new self-imposed reforms and freedoms. Not one of the characteristics of the colonial period (or any series of them) that might have been a cause of an independence movement did in fact cause the Spanish American independence movement, which was after all an event after the fact. For the pre-1810 period we can at best hope to discern the factors that might have produced independence under different circumstances but that in any case did contribute to shaping the new polities.

The search for meaningful clues in the late colonial period that might illumine the nature and problems of the new nations is complicated by the absence of a general consensus about the independence movement. In fact, an international congress on the causes and character of the independence movement held in 1949 concluded that given the then present state of investigations and knowledge it was impossible to formulate any such definitive general theory. In two decades the situation has not changed enough for us to offer one. Yet the Spanish American independence movement should be viewed as an event in the history of the Atlantic world. Both Spain and the colonies were very much in the mainstream of Atlantic civilization; and although the independence movement was strictly a civil war between Spain and its colonies, there was what might be called a spirit of the times that informed and helped shape both the late imperial system and the attitudes of the colonists.

The causes of independence are often included under four rubrics: the Enlightenment, the Bourbon reforms, the creole-peninsular controversy, and the late colonial revolts and protests. In the present chapter we shall be concerned with those aspects of the late colonial period that led some Americans, such as Francisco Miranda and Bernardo O'Higgins, to become active advocates of independence prior to the Napoleonic invasion of the Iberian peninsula and that led others to appreciate independence once that event took place. We shall also attempt to find clues to the nature of the new nations.

The Enlightenment

By the middle of the eighteenth century the European Enlightenment had come to mean the glorification of rationalism, a rationalism based not on the study of revelation and the ancient didactic tracts, but rather on facts gathered through the direct observation of nature. There has been an inclination to focus heavily on the political aspects of the Enlightenment—on the ideas of Locke, Montesquieu, Rousseau, and countless others—and lightly on other aspects of the movement. The Enlightenment was concerned, for instance, with philosophy, economics, and, very obviously, science. As Carl Becker has observed, the Enlightenment was "an international climate of opinion."[1] Except for the underlying fundamentals of a rationalism founded in the scientific method and a respect for man and his perfectability, this climate of opinion was not in general agreement on many things. In the political field there was strong support for both limited monarchy and enlightened despotism. There were thinkers impressed with Locke's conception of a society of individuals and others impressed with Rousseau's conception of a society of the people. In practical terms the difference between these two political theories could not have been greater; in fact constitutions were often designed to prevent advocates of the theory not in ascendancy at the moment from gaining control of the government. During the eighteenth century the Enlightenment caused many alterations in Spanish life and many critical changes in the imperial system. In a strict sense it had only an indirect effect on the Spanish American colonies in most cases, but the changes generated there by this new climate of opinion were both substantive and consequential. The European Enlightenment is the proper context in which to view the fall of the empire and the rise of the new nations.

The Enlightenment effectively got its start in Spain when the Bourbons occupied the throne at the beginning of the eighteenth century. Thereafter two broad stages can be discerned. The first extended to about the middle of the eighteenth century, and its most prominent figure was the Benedictine monk, Benito Jerónimo Feijóo. The second extended to the end of the century, and its most prominent and influential figure was Gaspar Melchor de Jovellanos. The central difference between the two periods is that the first recognized the concept of limited monarchy as it had developed over the centuries in Spain, and the second seemed to have lost track of this tradition as it bolstered the theories of enlightened despotism and strengthened the royal prerogatives. The second phase of the Enlightenment reached its highest development during the reign of Charles III (1759-1788) and was personified by his ministers Aranda, Campomanes, Cabarrús, and Floridablanca; by writers like Jovellanos; by economists such as Capmany, Ward, Asso, and Uztáriz; and by a prestigious group of first-rate scientists. The second phase was institutionalized and brought home to many people in the form of the famous Sociedades Económicos de los Amigos del País, the first one having been established in 1765. These were economic societies devoted to the rational pursuit of knowledge even in fields somewhat removed from economics. The societies not only heightened the Enlightenment in Spain, they disseminated it. Their efforts contributed to making Spain a leader in the world of science.

The men of the Enlightenment in Spain were clearly and quite effectively reformers. They reformed the economic system, the political system, the schools, the church, and the sciences. In a sense it is not unfair to think of them as liberals, much like their counterparts in the colonies. But this is misleading, since their reforms were designed to enhance the powers of the crown. Even the church reforms were not intended to undermine the place of the church in the Spanish system but were against antimonarchical tendencies, typified by the powerful and quite independent Jesuits. These reforms too were in the service of enlightened despotism. The only field in which the reformers were truly liberal was science. They were liberal in this field because science did not have immediate or even obvious proximate political overtones; and they were liberal, although often unwittingly, also because the new science, cartesianism, was a method of inquiry that led people to question sacred institutions in other fields.

But there is another field in which it is hardly possible to avoid calling the reformers liberal. The economics they followed was increasingly the liberal economics of the French physiocrats and Adam Smith. Thus Jovellanos could argue in 1795 against entailed estates–lay or religious–and the equally powerful institution of privilege, the sheepraisers' guild, (the *Mesta*), and at the same time for scientific agriculture. The Spanish reformers were exceedingly liberal in their economics, just as were many colonists at the same time; but this does not mean that they were liberal in their politics, for in practically all instances they were not. Smith's liberal economics followed quite naturally from and was perfectly consonant with Locke's individualist, property oriented conception of state and society. The conjugation of Smith and Locke with an admixture of ideas from several other Enlightenment thinkers resulted in the liberalism of the late eighteenth and early nineteenth century that inspired constitutions in Spain and America and that was so antithetical to Rousseauian democracy. The economics of this liberalism was by definition liberal, for it advocated a more open system than the previous ones, it was not based either on slave or serf labor, and theoretically it opposed monopoly and the domination of the economy by any estate or corporate power. Even in practical terms the new economics, as it became implemented at the end of the eighteenth and the beginning of the nineteenth century, was impressively liberal in many respects. But the politics, the liberal politics, that went along so easily with the liberal economics was emphatically conservative by both Rousseauian and modern standards. Combined, the liberal economics and the so-called liberal politics have had an enduring influence on the course of Western civilization. And it was this spirit of liberalism that pervaded the late colonial and early national periods in Spain and the colonies.

As a climate of opinion, a spirit, the Enlightenment could not be kept out of Spanish America by royal fiat, as the crown would have liked, or by such artificial barriers as the Inquisition and censorship. The colonists who comprised the active citizenry not only read the same books as their counterparts in Europe (although often clandestinely and sometimes by means of a lone, much used and prized copy) but discussed the same philosophic and practical issues. Spanish bureaucrats, foreign travelers, sailors from ships that had to make distress calls, sailors from the innumerable contraband ships, members of the foreign scientific expeditions that were permitted to visit the colonies during the late colonial period, Spanish and foreign merchants—all were potential sources of Enlightenment knowledge and approaches.

In the long run it was probably not the reading of a work by Locke, Montesquieu, Rousseau, or any of the other political philosophers, or the conversation with a foreigner who might have participated in the American or French revolutions, that gave the Enlightenment currency in the colonies and created an intellectual climate of opinion that would soon contribute to the consummation of an independence movement. The Enlightenment was too broad for that, and in the sense that it might be a challenge to royal absolutism and a colonial empire, its most revolutionary aspects were not necessarily in the field of political thought. Cartesian rationalism, a belief and faith in progress and in the perfectability of man, can be quite unsettling to an absolutist imperial system. And this can be translated into other forms than political treatises. It could, for instance, be expressed in fiction, and many Spanish American writers of fiction did, in fact, convey the tenets of the Enlightenment quite as effectively as if they had been writing political tracts.

As obviously important as Enlightenment thought was for the preparation of an intellectual climate hospitable to an independence movement so too was Enlightenment thinking, a way of thinking, of looking at things, that was very much incorporated into the colonial system by the end of the eighteenth century. It can be seen in the vigorous efforts at both economic and scientific development and progress. The crown sent several renowned scientists to the colonies. Outstanding among them were Fuasto and Juan José de Elhuyar and Baron Nordenflicht. The Elhuyar brothers were responsible for two important scientific missions to Mexico. Nordenflicht spent about twenty years in Peru, where he not only raised the level of science being practiced but inculcated modern scientific methods. The crown's interests were pragmatic rather than academic: It wanted increased revenues from the mining industry. Nevertheless, scores of young scientists in Mexico and Peru were being trained by celebrated instructors in the latest scientific techniques and methods. To them medieval scholasticism was every bit as alien as it was to European scientists. They were just as much a part of the mainstream of the Enlightenment as their European colleagues. They were a weighty factor in the generation of an Enlightenment climate of opinion in the colonies.

The pursuit of economic progress also contributed significantly to the presence of Enlightenment thinking. Between the early 1780s and 1812 about twelve economic societies, Sociedades Económicos de Amigos del País, modeled after the Madrid Society, were established in the colonies. Not all of them lasted long or were impressive in their accomplishments; and at least two, the Caracas Society, established in 1810, and the Buenos Aires Society, established in 1812, were actually political rather than economic societies. But the better ones were admirable advocates of rationalism and progress in their pursuit of economic development. They were also actively concerned with scientific progress. Perhaps the most important point about them is that their membership was comprised largely of the nonscientist, the noneconomist, and the nonpolitical theorist. Most of the members were merchants, agrarians, and bureaucrats. That is, the economic societies brought the Enlightenment home to a broad spectrum of the active citizenry, men who would soon play key roles in the independence movement and the new governments.

Another important source of the Enlightenment was the universities and even the high schools, the *colegios*. Spanish America possessed several excellent universities. During the eighteenth century their curricula were modernized, and while they might not have been teaching Rousseau, they were teaching Descartes and Newton, which in the long run was just as provocative and dangerous. The colonies were not in the vanguard of change. It took nearly a century after Descartes's death for cartesianism to find an open and secure place in the curricula. But once change was instituted and modernization became a reality new ideas were more quickly adopted. Newton's teachings were incorporated shortly after his death. Government officials often encouraged the process. During the final phase of the colonial period there were viceroys who directly influenced the reform of curricula, the incorporation of modern writers, and the establishment of Enlightenment institutions. By the last decades of empire there was practically no intellectual lag between Europe and the colonies.

By the end of the colonial period all the ingredients of the European Enlightenment were to be found in Spanish America. The colonists did not have to read a particular political tract—many of which the church, through the Inquisition, was trying unsuccessfully to keep out of the colonies—to come to its conclusions. Once a colonist was imbued with the Enlightenment, once he swam in the mainstream of the climate of opinion, once he was aware of what was going on in the revolutionary Western world (as was the case with thousands of colonists), he need not have troubled himself searching out Rousseau; there was inflammatory revolutionary doctrine right in the heart of the Spanish political tradition. The contractual theory of government and the concept of popular sovereignty had underpinned Spanish political theory centuries before the Enlightenment had its vogue, and they continued to do so while Locke, Montesquieu, and Rousseau were having their day. Both the contractual theory and the concept of popular sovereignty were integral components of medieval scholastic thought. They were already being absorbed into the Catalan way of life when Saint Thomas gave them respectability. They were popularized in Spain especially by Francisco Suárez (1548-1617). Suárez recognized the alienation of sovereignty to the prince; but he maintained that should the prince be incapable of exerting control, sovereignty would then revert to the people. Even laws would lose their legitimacy in the event of being unjust, too severe, or disavowed by a majority of the people. Clearly, in the proper context this might be the stuff of revolution, and it was good old respectable Spanish scholastic political theory.

That is, it was respectable until the middle of the eighteenth century when the Bourbons attempted to revitalize royal absolutism through the guise of enlightened despotism. Practically all education in the colonies was conducted by the church, and while the church taught the scientific principles of the Enlightenment it quite naturally did not teach the obviously revolutionary political principles of such thinkers as Rousseau. Rather, traditional scholastic political theory was taught in one form or another. The powerful Jesuits were especially interested in Suárez. For one thing, he too was a Jesuit, but more importantly the Jesuits consistently resisted regalist tendencies and tried to limit crown interference with the order. As the Bourbons began to centralize authority and establish a much tighter control over church activities and policies, the Jesuits became more and more attracted to Suárez's concepts of contractual government and popular sovereignty.

Even prior to the eighteenth century Suárez had been taught in the colonies, but with the Bourbons he had a revival. For instance, the University of Córdoba decided in 1730 to teach his doctrines exclusively. Mexico was quite Suárez oriented; there was even a chair in Suárezian theory at the University of Mexico. By the middle of the eighteenth century, when the Jesuits were practically at war with the crown—in Paraguay they would in fact soon fight colonial forces with arms—Suárez was being taught rather more than casually wherever Jesuits were to be found, which means throughout the colonies. It was for a variety of secondary reasons that the crown expelled the Jesuits from the colonies in 1767 and confiscated their enormous wealth. The principal reason, however, was that the Jesuits thwarted the crown's vigorous efforts at enlightened despotism and royal absolutism. And one way the Jesuits did this was by teaching Suárez in the colonies. Jesuit teaching was ended, and Jesuit philosophy was eliminated from the curricula.

But this did not keep Jesuit thought out of the colonies after 1767 any more than the Inquisition managed to keep out Rousseauian thought. In fact, it was even more difficult to excise Suárez because his thought was already known to a whole generation of students and was ingrained in the Spanish political tradition.

There is no real way of determining which political philosopher or philosophy had the greatest impact on late colonial Spanish America. Often when independence leaders spoke of the social contract and invoked the name of Rousseau they were for the moment forgetting the scandalous excesses of revolutionary Rousseauian democracy and were merely updating traditional Spanish thought as presented by Suárez. It is quite possible to speak of Rousseau in such a way that it would be difficult to distinguish him from Suárez. The great revolutionary period was one of ideas as well as action; and when in such times there is more than one political philosophy available, men tend to select the philosophy that reflects their personalities, habits, and desires. A society whose active citizenry is centrally bourgeois—as was the late colonial Spanish American—does not find satisfaction in Rousseau and his concept of mass democracy unless it does so selectively. That is, when the independence leaders needed philosophy to justify their predispositions they took what they wanted from the Enlightenment. Except in rare instances (for there were a few Rousseauian democrats around), no matter what terminology was employed one gets the impression that traditional Spanish political theory was being updated with the help of thinkers like Locke, Montesquieu, and Rousseau. The Spanish American bourgeois society was classically liberal in the Lockean mold prior to independence, and after justifying its steps toward independence with Rousseau and Suárez, it fast became Lockean liberal again. Governments dedicated to law and order, to the protection of personal property, and to the glorification of the individual were established everywhere.

The Bourbon Reforms

With a keen awareness of the reforms being carried out by their French cousins, the Spanish Bourbons determined to revamp and revitalize the colonial system. The reforms were designed to enhance royal prerogatives and further royal absolutism, to increase revenues from the colonies, to protect the empire from foreign encroachment, and to satisfy some of the complaints voiced by the colonists that might lead to insurrection. Altogether the reforms reflected the crown's conception of enlightened despotism. The reforms were part and parcel of the Enlightenment, and they had much to do with preparing the way for an easy acceptance of independence on the part of many colonists.

Free Trade

Apart from the expulsion of the Jesuits the most famous of the Bourbon reforms was the freedom of trade decree of 1778. It permitted thirteen Spanish ports to trade directly with all important ports in the Spanish American colonies except Veracruz, Mexico, and La Guayra, Venezuela, which were included in 1789. The many Spanish American ports authorized to participate in the trans-Atlantic trade were also permitted generally to trade among themselves. The colonial trade monopoly headed up by the Seville-Cádiz merchants was thus ended. During the first decade of the decree there was prodigious expansion of trade in the colonies, at least according to official figures. Actually the new system was doing a good deal to frustrate the vast and lucrative contraband network which crisscrossed the colonies. But, at any rate, this increased legal trade meant more money for the royal coffers. The decree also reduced some tariffs and in general placed emphasis on facilitating commerce within the empire. Expanding trade and breaking the Seville-Cádiz merchant monopoly contributed to the creation of a new class of merchants dependent on the open system for their success. It is often suggested that the new trade regulations heightened the desire of merchant and colonist alike for further easy access to European and American goods, that the appetites of both had been whetted to the point of leading them to independence. This is simply not true.

When the Spaniards spoke of free trade they were not advocating Smithian laissez faire economics. They were introducing certain liberal economic features in order to strengthen, not weaken, the mercantile system. At the same moment that trade was expanded the crown established the famous and powerful tobacco monopoly, the *estanco*. The liberal trade regulations that were established did not treat everyone kindly. In many regions nascent industries were overcome by the newly arrived cheap European goods. Those adversely affected might just choose independence, once the subject was broached, precisely in order to escape the new liberal economics. Many merchants also were adversely affected by the new regulations, some being forced out of their customary and traditionally secure positions by the nouveaux riches, others being driven to alternative endeavors. However, these merchants would likely favor the colonial system and oppose independence. And, in fact, during independence the powerful merchant community did split—and not always according to a recognizable pattern. It is plain that a great majority of the peninsular merchants were royalists, but there are outstanding examples of creole merchants in either camp.

The new trade regulations made it patently clear to many influential colonists that they needed a political economy of their own design. In some cases it was obvious that less, not more, free trade was necessary for the economic health of a particular colony. Actually, some regions had been treated to a good deal of free trade even before the 1778 decree, and they had not always liked the results. The question of freedom of trade after 1778—whether to have more or less of it—was pertinent to independence on a general rather than specific level. That is, the desire for more or less freedom of trade varied according to the moment. The real, fundamental question was who should decide the issue generally; and while some Spanish Americans must have thought prior to 1810 that they should, it appears that the great majority of active citizens in the colonies did not come to this conclusion until after the independence movement had gotten under way—that is, until after the colonists were doing this anyway.

The Chileans, for instance, promulgated a free trade decree of their own shortly after the establishment of the first national junta in September 1810. Since their decree was one of the first, it is often cited as evidence that obviously the Spanish Americans coveted an expanded trade enough to strike out for independence. Apart from the fact that many merchants, including creoles, were royalists, the February 1811 free trade decree of Chile incorporated a quite protectionist approach. Certain items could not be imported at all. Others might be excluded in the future in order to promote the country's industry. Certain articles of war were permitted tariff-free entrance into the country for a year and a half. The article dealing with the war items also mentioned that under the same conditions the implements and machines for the manufacture or weaving of hemp, linen, cotton, and wool could be introduced. It is unlikely that all members of the junta considered the production of hemp, linen, cotton, and wool limited strictly or even primarily to the question of military defense. The month before the decree was announced a leading government official, José Santiago Portales, presented to the junta an analysis of the economic, cultural and political situation of Chile, in which he observed that free trade of itself would leave Chile at an international disadvantage and that therefore its manufacturing and agricultural base should be developed. He counseled that manufactures competitive with European products should be emphasized, and singled out the production of linen. The free trade decree did in fact give linen production special attention.

The point is that the Chileans wanted both to trade with whomever they so desired and to protect and promote their own industrial and agricultural base. This was true of other Spanish Americans as well. For instance, the province of Buenos Aires, Argentina, promulgated its first general tariff in January 1822. It established a basic rate of 15 percent ad valorem on overseas imports. However, a number of needed items, such as agricultural tools and mining machinery, were subject to only a 5 percent tariff. Foreign products that competed with local goods—such as sugar, coffee, cocoa, yerba maté, tea, and foodstuffs —were subject to a 20 percent tariff. Goods imported from other provinces of the Argentine confederation were generally subject to only a 4 percent ad valorem tariff. Thus, like the Chilean decree of 1811 this one incorporated protection within the broad concept of free trade. The 1822 tariff protected the wine and brandy industries of the provinces of Mendoza and San Juan and the sugar industry of Tucumán. This meant that the consumers in Buenos Aires were required to support Argentine provincial industry at their own expense. Both the Chilean and Argentine trade decrees protected specified industries from foreign competition, something the liberal trade regulations of the late colonial period did not always do.

It is clear that the colonists had less need of free trade than of a political economy attentive to the requirements of individual regions;

and this is precisely what they got with independence. Economics did not cause independence, but the obvious need for a political economy of their own design induced many Spanish Americans to appreciate it once it came.

The Intendancy System

In their attempts to rationalize the administration of the empire the Bourbon monarchs instituted several eventful changes designed to centralize control. One of them was the addition of two new viceroyalties–New Granada in 1717 and Río de la Plata in 1776. Following the same line of reasoning, the intendancy system was established, first in Cuba during the 1760s and then in the rest of the colonies. The intendants, almost always peninsulars, replaced previous provincial governors but enjoyed far greater powers than their predecessors. In their provinces they were given control of justice, general governmental administration, finance, and war. They were subordinate to the viceroy but in certain respects (such as financial matters) enjoyed some independence of him. And, in fact, some viceroys came to oppose the intendant system vigorously.

Overall the intendants had a noteworthy effect on late colonial life. In many local regions they restored economies and won approval from the residents. For a long time the *cabildos* of most provincial regions had become less than dynamic institutions of government. For instance, the Chilean government tried to sell two positions of town councilman in the Concepción *cabildo*. It set a price of 200 pesos; two merchants each bid 140 pesos (the highest bids received), and the government decided to accept. There were literally hundreds of people who could have raised the 200 pesos if they had desired a seat on the town council of the capital of the south. In some regions the intendants, by injecting new economic life into the municipalities, made the *cabildos* more energetic institutions. But by the same token, precisely because they interfered so directly in the affairs of *cabildos* they may have made some positions even less desirable than they had been previously and at the same time may have antagonized many influential local residents. Even prior to the creation of the intendancy system there existed provincial officials who could preside over the sessions and activities of the *cabildos*. But their positions were not designed to be so powerful as those of the intendants.

Again the Concepción case is instructive. The intendancy of Concepción—that is, the effective south of Chile—was created in 1786. Between 1789 and1796 the intendant waged an intensive legal battle to force members of two leading families out of the town council. His reason was that the families were too heavily represented in the council. As a result of the intendant's strenuous efforts, Francisco Javier Manzanos, a powerful creole merchant, was forced off the Concepción town council. But the intendant had also singled out the important landowning Puga family as having too great a representation in the *cabildo.* The intendant must have been a confident fellow, for he had thus taken on two of the south's leading families. A ruling by the captain general in 1796 contradicted the intendant's position, but the damage had been done.

The intendant of the south of Chile was an outsider and a peninsular, a European Spaniard. Previously the provincial figure closest to the intendant in power in the south of Chile was the corregidor. During the period prior to the creation of the intendancy system the corregidors had been creoles and residents of the region. This was often the case throughout the colonies. But now there was a new and powerful official who was an intruder upon local societies, societies in which the creole oligarchy was accustomed to considerable freedom of action. The actions of the intendant of Concepción could not have endeared him to these future creole leaders of independence. By nature the intendants were meddlers in local affairs, and we may assume that the Concepción situation was not at all rare for Spanish America as a whole.

It is clear that in many places the intendants did a great deal of good; however in others they were rendered ineffectual by jealous central authorities. Perhaps their most enduring contribution was to alienate sectors of the creole population who would shortly have the opportunity of deciding whether or not to strike out for independence.

The Creole Military

One of the consequential Bourbon reforms was the creation of creole regular army units and the expansion of the creole militia, both with creole officers. To garrison the colonies effectively with peninsular troops against the eventuality of foreign invasion and even local social unrest would have required an enormous outlay of money just at the time the crown was reforming the imperial system to produce increased revenues. Doubtless the crown would have felt more secure with an all peninsular army and officialdom, but its shaken financial position limited the options. Colonial armies were created, and militia units were greatly enlarged, incorporating tens of thousands of part-time soldiers. Those in the militia were entitled to the same *fuero* (the privilege of special military jurisdiction for themselves and their families) enjoyed by the regular army personnel. Many creoles would have joined the militia for no other reason than to take themselves outside the purview of the civil courts, but there were also other attractions. The creoles were honored by the new liberal policy and were quick to take advantage of it. It was for many a form of recognition. The uniform was as great an attraction then as it is now for some people. In the principal urban centers the creoles were proud that they were finally to be admitted into the ranks of military officialdom and to share a broad range of obvious privileges with their peninsular colleagues. In the many frontier and near-frontier regions creoles were equally pleased to see the formation of local militia units with themselves as the officers. Had additional peninsular troops and officers been placed in these regions the creoles would have faced increased competition in their quest for social dominance. Peninsular officers, after all, were very attractive figures, especially to the young creole ladies. Now the creoles became the officers and got the uniforms. A potential social impediment had been eliminated in many places.

While enacting a reform that was entirely appealing to the creole upper classes, the crown was unwittingly preparing the future patriot armies. By the early nineteenth century thousands of organized troops could be called out at a moment's notice. The officers were creoles, many of whom would opt for independence. The troops often were the employees of the officers, especially in the rural regions.

A critical ingredient for a successful independence movement had thus been supplied by the crown.

Church Reforms

For centuries the church had been relatively unhindered in its efforts to acquire vast economic wealth and exert influence at all levels of colonial life. The Bourbon reformers, especially the count of Campomanes and the count of Floridablanca, considered the church a clear obstacle in their plan to invigorate both royal absolutism and the colonial economy. Thus just at the time the crown was strengthening the military *fuero*—an indication of where it chose to place its trust—it was curtailing the church *fuero*. However, except in one significant instance, the reformers' efforts to limit ecclesiastic political power in the colonies were largely undermined after Charles III died. That exception was the crown's determination to destroy the political and economic power of the Jesuits. They were expelled in 1767, and their extensive economic assets were sold at public auction, with the proceeds going to the royal treasury. A major stumbling block to royal absolutism was thus eliminated, and the crown became notably richer in the process. Several of the Jesuits-in-exile became prominent promoters of complete independence of the colonies from Spain. The most famous of them was Juan Pablo Viscardo, who published his *Letter to Spanish Americans* during the last decade of the eighteenth century. It was a bitter denunciation of three centuries of Spanish rule, and it concluded by urging the Spanish Americans to revolt and establish their independence. While it does not appear that the exiled Jesuits seriously influenced the independence movement, there can be no doubt that they must have caused some colonists to question the sanctity of the imperial system.

The secular hierarchy was not overly disturbed by such crown reforms, since they were directed at the regular orders, with whom they felt competition. But some members of the regular and secular clergy did become partisans of independence a while before the movement actually commenced. For instance, young Bernardo O'Higgins, already a convinced separatist, came into contact with two Spanish American clerics in Spain who favored independence just at the beginning of the eighteenth century. One was Juan Pablo Fretes, Argentine by birth, but later canon of the Cathedral of Santiago and president of Chile's first national congress. Probably O'Higgins was merely confirmed in his own views, but it must be assumed that other creoles who were on the fence about the matter were pushed a bit in the direction of independence by such clerics and their attitudes.

An economic reform instituted at the end of the colonial period did encourage many clergymen to favor independence. Throughout the colonial period it had been traditional for the rich to leave a legacy, often a substantial one, for the creation of a pious work or chantry. The pious works came to possess great sums of money, which the church made a practice of loaning out to lay citizens at the standard 5 percent interest. It was primarily through this source of capital, always being renewed by new legacies, that the church became the single leading credit institution in the colonies. The chantries were endowments for the saying of masses for someone's soul. Generally, throughout the colonies, parish priests depended directly on the chantries as a supplement for their meager incomes. In some regions practically the entire secular clergy depended on these endowments for their income. Chantries were also used as a source of credit by the church. In 1804 the crown expropriated all land and capital belonging to the pious works and chantries.

As a result of its unsuccessful warfaring activities during the late eighteenth century the Spanish government chose to issue paper currency to cover its debts. Almost immediately this paper depreciated to half its par value. At war with Great Britain in 1804, Spain had to resort to extreme financial measures. The alienation of the wealth pertaining to the pious works and chantries was designed to raise specie with which to cover the paper currency already issued in Spain.

Limiting the church's banking operations was certainly a reform, but it was one that antagonized laymen and clergymen alike. We have already spoken of the importance of church capital to the colonial economy. The crown's actions in 1804 meant the calling in of loans based on the pious works and chantries. In some colonies, such as Mexico, the very existence of a functioning economy was thus threatened. Somewhere around ten or twelve million pesos were collected by the Caja de Consolidación from Mexico alone by 1809 when the program was terminated. There were regions in the colonies in which the crown's efforts never really got underfoot, and therefore few people were antagonized. Where its efforts were successful, as in Mexico, important segments of society were estranged from the colonial system. This meant merchant and landowner alike, for both were quite often deeply in debt to the church. Having to pay up all at once was indeed an insufferable shock.

In colonies such as Mexico, where the crown's efforts were impressive, it was probably the lower secular clergy, the parish priests, who suffered the deepest economic dislocations. It is not surprising that by 1810 many parish priests were either decided advocates of independence or were easy converts once the movement got under way.

These were the church reforms that contributed to the independence of Spanish America. Yet some clergymen would have become advocates of independence even were there no reforms. Many clergymen, like Hidalgo of Mexico, were caught up in the momentum of the Enlightenment and were reading the most modern and provocative works. They surely would have come to question the validity and efficacy of the colonial system in their own good time.

The Creole-Peninsular Controversy

The controversy between creoles and peninsulars for public office has long been considered one of the chief causes of the independence movement. It is a theme that has become ubiquitous in our literature. Although there was no legal distinction between creoles and peninsulars for public office, it is clear that European-born Spaniards were given preference in the highest decision-making posts. Once the independence movement commenced liberal writers often seized upon this fact of colonial life to justify the actions of the creoles. In the 1820s a Chilean newspaper actually attributed independence to the preferential treatment accorded peninsulars in the selection of public officials. There can be no doubt that a controversy existed and that it encouraged some creoles toward independence. In some colonies creoles achieved all but the very highest positions–including that of intendant, which generally was unavailable to them–but in other colonies peninsulars dominated the bureaucracy. Thus at the moment the first national junta was created in Santiago in September 1810 the interim governor and captain general was a creole, although a titled aristocrat; so too were the bishop-elect of Santiago, two judges of the royal *audiencia*, the superintendent of the royal mint, the administrator of the customs house, and the *asesor* (the chief counsel in the colony). The upper bureaucracy was very much peopled by creoles in Chile by the end of the colonial period. On the other hand, at one point during the final colonial period the upper bureaucracy of Mexico was very much peninsular. For instance, contrary to the situation in Chile, the superintendent of the mint, the administrator of the customs house, and the chief counsel of the realm were all peninsulars.

In fact, just as the creoles were flexing their economic muscles the crown instituted a less equitable policy in the selection of public officials. Whatever the situation had been before (and there is no certainty as to what this was) it is clear that during the final phase of empire there was no fundamental social difference between peninsulars and creoles in the colonies. Peninsulars belonged to whatever social grouping they could get into with their credentials. By the last decades of the eighteenth century creoles competed with and often superseded peninsulars even in the economic areas in which the Europeans had concentrated, such as trade. What is more, the colonies witnessed a significant immigration of Basques during the eighteenth century. These were generally hardworking, highly industrious, and quickly successful newcomers. By 1767 many of them had earned substantial fortunes, enough to purchase Jesuit estates. During the last decades of the century many Basques were to be found in local town councils. Thus peninsulars often shared political power with the creoles at the local level of government. But the Basques often married creoles, and by the last decade of the century their sons were replacing them in the town councils—and the sons were generally creoles. These and other successful creoles resented the creation of a local officer, the intendant, who was generally a peninsular. Many also resented crown policy of not appointing creoles to the very highest posts.

The crown contributed to the growing creole disenchantment by purposely favoring peninsulars for some positions during the final decades of the colonial period. Minister of the Indies José de Gálvez had a striking predilection for European bureaucrats. For instance, in about 1769 the most important *audiencia* in Mexico was comprised of six creole superior judges out of a possible seven. There were then two lesser creole judges also, and these judges generally became the superior judges. Only a decade later there were four creole superior judges and no creole lesser judges. Later there were only three creoles among the eleven members of the upper court. Gálvez's policy was clearly working and doubtless antagonizing innumerable creoles, Spanish Americans who in ever increasing numbers sat at the top of the social and economic ladders in the colonies.

During the last decades of the eighteenth century creoles were successful, confident, and assertive. The crown's preference, inspired in part by Minister Gálvez, for Europeans in certain critical posts and the creation of the intendancy system headed up by peninsulars must be considered factors which alienated creoles from the imperial system and helped prepare a climate of opinion hospitable to independence once the opportunity arose.

The Late Colonial Revolts and Protests

As little as we know about many aspects of colonial life we know even less about the colonial revolts and protests that shook the foundations of the empire and encouraged the Bourbon monarchs to rationalize the system and tighten control. The revolts, some major and others minor, have received precious little attention from professional historians. We need to know much more about them before meaningful conclusions may be drawn. Yet it is plain that the colonial system was not structurally sound and that society was not entirely somnolent. Under the pressures of a surprisingly wide variety of circumstances the colonists clearly were willing to take matters into their own hands and contest royal officials. The revolts and protests may be divided into three general categories: those with deep political origins and overtones, those with social origins and overtones, and those with civil origins and overtones.

The Political Revolts

The political revolts were few and conspicuously unsuccessful. The most famous were those fomented by the Venezuelan precursor of Spanish American independence, Francisco Miranda. Miranda fought in both the American and French revolutions and devoted considerable time and energy to convincing first the British and then the North Americans to sponsor a liberating invasion of the colonies. In 1806 he actually made two landings at northern South America. His miniature expeditionary force could not support his grandiose plans. Miranda had meant to liberate the colonies, but the colonists were not yet impressed with such thoughts.

There were also liberating plans developed within the colonies, but these did not fare better. For instance, in 1780 Chile witnessed the conspiracy of the Tres Antonios. This stillborn revolt was fraught with the deepest political meaning and was hardly casual in its intentions. Two Frenchmen, Antonio Gramusset and Antonio Berney, had enlisted the aid of one of Chile's most prominent citizens, José Antonio de Rojas, in a plan to establish a republican government based on an inclusive electoral process. Social classes were to be eliminated and slavery abolished. A major program of agrarian reform was included in their plans, along with a broad policy of free trade with the world at large. The three Antonios had conjured up one of the most democratic conspiracies in Spanish American history up to the middle of the nineteenth century. But, unfortunately for those involved, it was ill-supported, ineffectual, and actually a conspiracy (as it is called) rather than a full-fledged rebellion.

The few Mirandas and Antonios, the ones with the truly sophisticated thoughts, were as yet extraneous to the body politic they wished to convert.

The Social Revolts

The social revolts were distinctly more impressive in dimension and effect. They were also more threatening to the colonial system. The most famous of them was the revolt of Túpac Amaru II, which also began in 1780. José Gabriel Condorcanqui Noguera was an educated *mestizo* (a man of mixed Indian and white blood) and a landowner of note. Through inheritance and official approval he was a *cacique*, a man responsible for collecting the annual tribute owed by the Indians in his charge and for supervising their forced work schedules. *Caciques* also had criminal jurisdiction within their regions for minor cases. However, the *caciques* were themselves relatively minor officials. The real authority over the Indians at the provincial and local level was the corregidor. No one exploited anyone during the colonial period as much as the corregidors exploited the Indians, often working hand in hand with the local *caciques*. José Gabriel was one of the few *caciques* who developed a social consciousness, who was deeply troubled by the outrageous exploitation he witnessed and was willing to do something about it. Sometime during the 1770s he took the name Túpac Amaru II, suggesting his supposed direct lineage from the great Inca monarch of the same name.

Early in November 1780 Túpac Amaru, with a few followers, seized the notorious corregidor of the province of Tinta, Peru, and forced him to sign over arms, ammunition, and money. The corregidor was then constrained to issue an order demanding that all residents of the province appear at the town of Tungasuca within twenty-four hours. Thousands of people showed up, and in their presence the corregidor was executed. Túpac Amaru insisted that he was carrying out a royal order which called for the execution and suppressed the *alcabala* (local sales tax), the *derechos de aduanas* (customs duties), and the *mita* (enforced labor of the Indians in the mines). The thousands assembled actually thought they were witnessing the compliance of a royal order. Túpac Amaru gathered an army and began marching through the countryside, destroying the detested *obrajes* (textile sweatshops) and the houses of the corregidors, who were quick to flee.

News of the rebellion spread rapidly throughout the Andean region, and a wave of Indian uprisings ensued. A full-blown race war was now in progress. Before it ended–in 1781 in most places–some estimates suggest that one hundred thousand people lost their lives. Before Túpac Amaru II was captured and executed in the spring of 1781, the viceroy of Peru created a Junta Extraordinaria to look into the causes of the rebellion. It concluded that the system of *repartimiento*, by which the corregidors force-sold goods to the Indians–often whether they needed them or not, and at unreasonable prices–was the central Indian complaint and cause of the rebellion. It therefore abolished the *repartimiento*; however, the *mita* was continued. Eventually the corregidor system itself was abolished and replaced by one of intendants. A special *audiencia* was established at Cuzco for the purpose of hearing Indian grievances.

If the crown had not realized it before–and it had been told so in official reports–it certainly knew as a result of Túpac Amaru's rebellion that reform was urgently required in the administration of Indian life. And reforms were in fact taken, but they were designed not so much to enhance the Indians' life as to prevent rebellion and guarantee a steady source of cheap labor for colonists and crown alike. The rebellion had other lessons. It demonstrated loudly and clearly that masses of Indians would fight, and would do so bitterly and effectively. Túpac Amaru's relatives continued the rebellion for a while after his death and brought its virulence home to colonists in many regions throughout the Andean colonies. All this occurred before the French Revolution and its reign of terror. Those creoles who had been reading radical democratic literature now could see firsthand how much more comfortable were other theories of government and society. Quite a few creoles must have been put off by the whole occurrence.

It is difficult to gauge the importance of the rebellion on the future independence movement. The simple fact remains that Indians fought on both sides of that movement, some with the crown and some against it. There seems to be no recognizable pattern of choice. Indians generally took the side supported by their local priest or *cacique*, and their choice was not always directly related to the degree of Indian exploitation. Often Indians fought with the occupying forces, regardless of who they were.

The Civil Protests

The most consequential of the colonial uprisings were the civil protests, the ones that seem to have made the least lasting impression. They occurred all during the colonial period and continued right up to the time of independence. They were very much part and parcel of the colonial tradition. In fact, the independence movement stemmed directly and naturally from this tradition. The civil revolts were generally not founded on any special political theory. They were specific reactions to specific grievances, and they followed patterns of action established over the centuries. The following examples are intended to show how widespread and socially accepted these civil protests were.

To the north of Mexico City lies a mountain range famous for silver production. Its capital is Guanajuato, a center of the 1810 Indian rebellion (which will be discussed in Chapter 3). During the 1760s Guanajuato suffered severe revolts. In protest against new taxes on wheat, flour, meat, and wood and against the inferior product marketed by the newly created tobacco monopolists, about six thousand people stormed the royal treasury on one occasion. In their rage they shouted "Long live the King! Death to bad government!"[2] As was typical of the civil protests, the people were carefully loyal to the king. One of the causes of this protest was the recent creation of a militia in which they might have to serve. As a result of the protest, plans for the militia were abandoned. No one was imprisoned or otherwise punished. A more threatening protest occurred the following year because of the expulsion of the Jesuits. For three days mobs controlled the streets of Guanajuato in protest of the expulsion. This protest was not limited to Guanajuato alone. It was considered a full-fledged revolt by the authorities. The royal representative in Mexico, *visitador* José de Gálvez, soon to be minister of the Indies, had 9 of the rebels hanged and 31 imprisoned for life. Another 148 were given prison sentences of six to ten years.

In New Granada another royal *visitador* exemplified the Bourbon rationalization of the colonial system. He also raised taxes and applied new ones. In 1781 a riot against the taxes and higher prices broke out at Socorro, near Bogotá. Several thousand men prepared to march on the capital of the viceroyalty to protest taxes and monopolies. They took the name *comuneros*, obviously declaring kinship to the famous Spanish municipal rebellion of the 1520s. In June royal officials signed an agreement with the *comuneros* whereby new taxes and monopolies would be abolished and creoles would be given additional positions in government. The viceroy and the *visitador*, who had not participated in the agreement, denounced it. So far the *comunero* movement was largely a creole venture. But at this juncture a smaller rebellion, led by an Indian inspired by the Túpac Amaru revolt, developed among the indigenous population. It scared colonial officials and creoles alike. An army soon put down the revolts of the *comuneros* and the Indians. Spanish America was certainly not sleeping during the last decades of the eighteenth century.

The revolts of the *comuneros* in New Granada and the Mexicans in Guanajuato were in their own way a bit spectacular. Yet there were other civil protests that were much less spectacular and at the same time more ominous. One of them occurred in the town of Concepción, Chile, in 1794. In that year the *cabildo* of Concepción held what it called a *cabildo pleno*, comprised of the town council, the *vecindario* (some of the local residents), and other invited individuals. It was really, as the *audiencia* later noted, a *cabildo abierto*, an open *cabildo*. The *cabildo abierto* addressed a letter to the captain general of Chile arguing that a special tax that the *audiencia* wanted to extend was unfair and should be terminated. The problem was the negative trade balance Chile had long had with Peru. A five-year special tax had been established to improve the situation. Every hundredweight of domestic produce exported to Lima or intermediary ports was taxed one-half *real*. The *audiencia* had decreed the extension of the tax beyond the original five years. Now the *cabildo abierto* presented several technical arguments to show why the *audiencia* should not continue the extension and, for that matter, why the tax should not have been established in the first place. Two of the arguments are especially interesting. The southerners observed that such taxes, according to law, were not to be imposed without a hearing from the municipal attorneys. This was an argument of no taxation without representation. What is more, they argued, far from aiding the trade balance, the tax actually ended in destroying southern trade while increasing Santiago's trade. The economic aspects of this situation properly belong to a study of the economic origins of Spanish American federalism. What is important here is that the southerners were complaining against what they considered the invidious actions of the central region, the Santiago-Valparaíso axis. The *cabildo* pointed out that only the *cabildo* of Santiago and the commercial community of that capital had been consulted about establishing the tax, and the southerners well understood that the interests of the capital's *cabildo* and commercial community were different from Concepción's interests.

This last argument is more than just a question of the existence of a disturbing tax; it is a question of just who is to establish such things. Concepción was not complaining against the tax *qua* tax but against the right of the central region to impose it upon the south. Although Concepción's position was not perfect in a legal sense, it was justified by the traditional interpretation of the rights of municipalities. It appeared to the residents of the southern capital—as it did to colonists throughout the colonies at about the same time—that the rules of empire were not being followed due to the insistence of the imperial administration and that consequently the colonists were being placed at a serious disadvantage.

If the Concepción community had thought it could solve its tax problem by writing to the captain general of Chile, it was in for quite a shock. There does not seem to be an answer from the captain general, but there is one from the *audiencia*. In September 1795 it sent a severe reprimand of the *cabildo abierto* to the intendant of Concepción. He was ordered to convene another *cabildo abierto* and tell its members of the displeasure and surprise the letter had caused the *audiencia*. Particularly distressing was "the liberty, and haughtiness noted in various of its clauses." To prevent such occurrences in the future the intendant was ordered to take precautions to insure that such groups of people did not meet, even under the pretext of a *cabildo abierto*, without express license from the *audiencia* or the supreme government. The appeal of the *cabildo abierto* was denied.

Two fundamental rights of municipalities were thus encumbered. One was the matter of taxation without representation. According to tradition the municipalities had a right to a hearing before taxes were established by the central authorities. By its actions the *audiencia* was effectively denying this. The other was the right of the town councils to convene the more inclusive *cabildo abierto* and direct appeals to higher authorities. The *audiencia* had affronted a great Spanish American tradition. Because of the importance of the *cabildos abiertos* during the independence movement in general it is easy to picture a bit more democracy in the institution of the *cabildo* and the *cabildo abierto* than actually existed. Nevertheless, both were familiar and cherished institutions. Just a decade and a half prior to the start of the Chilean independence movement the *audiencia's* actions must have impressed some as provocative.

Such events as these have gone relatively unnoticed in our appreciation of the colonial period. With order and calm the residents of a provincial capital—just as the residents of the more important capitals—from time to time resorted to entirely Spanish procedures to redress grievances. The heart of the Spanish political system was the municipality; and though the municipalities did nothing extravagant for a long while during the colonial period, with the Bourbon reforms they seemed to become more assertive. Not only would the *cabildo* of Concepción challenge the *audiencia*, unsuccessfully now, but in the near future it would challenge Joseph Bonaparte and then Santiago too. When Napoleon dethroned Ferdinand and replaced him with Joseph, the *cabildos* in many parts of the colonies became *cabildos abiertos* and took the first steps toward independence. They were following a Spanish procedure and in fact an example visible at that very moment in Spain itself.

The civil protests indicate that colonists were aware of their rights and willing to take matters into their own hands at times. Certainly some people involved in the protests must have come to question the desirability of empire and the efficacy of the colonial system. And one should bear in mind that the protests took place during the Enlightenment, a time of intellectual stimulation. Yet, as we have noted, if one were inclined to question the colonial system he could do so quite within the context of Spanish political theory and procedure. The *audiencia* of Chile thought the *cabildo* of Concepción disobedient. Given the time and place, the ideas that were circulating freely, and the outside forces that were soon to act, the protest of the vested interests of the south of Chile were more threatening to the colonial system than the more spectacular Guanajuato flare-ups.

However, one is always confronted by the plain fact that none of the ideas we have mentioned, none of the aspects of the colonial system that might have or properly should have caused independence, and none of the late revolts and protests did actually cause independence. If Napoleon's actions of 1807 and 1808 had not occurred, there is good reason to believe that the Bourbon reforms might have taken effect and accomplished their goals and that an independence movement might not have taken place for quite some time. In fact, even the colonial revolts and protests might have worked in the behalf of an enduring empire by generating a flexibility and safety-valve effect not envisioned by the crown.

The Actual Cause of Independence

There was an independence movement in the Caribbean even before Napoleon invaded the Iberian peninsula. During the temporary peace established by the Treaty of Amiens between France and Britain (to which Spain became a party, and in the process recognized its loss of Trinidad) Napoleon shipped twenty thousand troops to Saint-Domingue in an attempt to reanimate the French empire in America. The commander of the French forces, Napoleon's brother-in-law, General Leclerc, prepared to restore slavery—a rude shock to the black population that had won its freedom through a bloody and savage revolution during the 1790s. Whites and then mulattoes had been driven out of the country. It was a slave revolt, one that sent a shiver of fear down the spines of a good many whites in neighboring colonies and caused some of them, especially in Puerto Rico and Cuba, to maintain a fierce allegiance to Spain. The emergent black leader was Toussaint L'Ouverture, a former slave. Leclerc made a prisoner of him and sent him off to France, where he shortly died. A black revolt against the French was soon led by Jean Jacques Dessalines. Because of Napoleon's pressing commitments in Europe and a raging yellow fever epidemic in the colony, the French were defeated and Saint-Domingue became an independent state called Haiti in 1804. Haiti was thus the first colony south of the United States to achieve independence.

One of the reasons that Napoleon's continental plan to isolate Britain from the rest of Europe did not function well was that Britain had enjoyed a special protective relationship with Portugal for centuries and now freely docked ships at Lisbon. To plug the gap Napoleon, with Spanish support, sent a major French expedition under Marshall Andoche Junot through the peninsula to Portugal in 1807. The Portuguese royal court, including the mad queen Maria I, Prince Regent João, and thousands of nobles, boarded ships for Brazil. That colony's independence movement was postponed for a decade and a half because it now became the seat of the Portuguese empire.

In return for their support of the French invasion of Portugal the Spaniards were supposed to receive certain benefits. Instead, Napoleon occupied a portion of Spain. Charles IV moved his court out of Madrid to Aranjuez in an attempt to put some distance between him and the French armies. The Spanish army was not satisfied with the turn of events; it forced Charles to abdicate in favor of his son, who became Ferdinand VII. Ferdinand was immediately popular with the Spaniards but not with the French. Napoleon refused to recognize either Charles or Ferdinand as king of Spain. He managed to get both to meet with him at Bayonne, where he forced them to abdicate. Early in May he placed his brother Joseph, who had been king of Naples, on the Spanish throne. Even before final arrangements were announced at Bayonne, Spanish civilians were engaging French troops in Madrid. It was a bloody confrontation on that day of May 2, 1808, the day the Spanish war of independence began. Juntas came into existence in many parts of Spain to organize the war effort and govern in the absence of the lawful monarch. In September 1808 the many juntas joined together and established a central junta in Seville, often referred to as the *suprema*. It attempted to win the support of the Spanish American colonies, which it generally achieved. In 1810, however, the French took Seville, and the *suprema* was forced to flee. It got to Cádiz, where it was replaced by a Council of Regency, which began to rule in the name of Ferdinand VII. The regency called for the convening of a *Cortes*, to which the colonies were invited to send delegates.

The colonies did not belong to Spain but to the crown of Castile. As juntas sprang up in Spain to govern in the name of Ferdinand, so too did they in the colonies, and with perfect logic. Between 1810 and 1814, when Ferdinand was restored to the throne and proclaimed the reestablishment of royal absolutism, several of the colonies had grown decidedly accustomed to governing themselves and were manifestly prejudiced toward the reforms they had instituted during their self-rule.

With the restoration of Ferdinand they were ready to fight for their official independence.

This is how the Spanish American independence movement commenced. Without the events in the Iberian peninsula there is every reason to believe the empire would have been much longer lived. The Spanish American reactions to the Iberian events will be discussed shortly. Before doing so, one further aspect of the colonial system needs to be considered–its patrimonial nature.

Disruption of the Patrimonial System

Lately historians have become increasingly impressed with the viability of the general theories which inform other disciplines and so handily provide a framework within which to analyze societies. Marxist historians naturally have always had a general theory to comfort them through the rigors of research and analysis. But the non-Marxist historians have not been quite so blessed. Now they are turning to psychology, economics, and sociology, among others, to perceive applicable general theories. As a result certain theories of Max Weber have come into vogue among some historians. The great sociologist offered many alluring theories, including that of political domination always occurring in three central forms: the charismatic, the traditional, and the legal. Weber made it clear that he was speaking of theoretical models which never occurred in their pure form. One of the forms of traditional domination is patrimonialism. In traditional domination, "the object of obedience is the personal authority of the individual which he enjoys by virtue of his traditional status." Thus the relationship of the ruler's administrative staff to him is not determined by the "impersonal obligation of office, but personal loyalty to the chief."[3] When the administrative staff, including the military force, is completely under the personal control of the ruler, the traditional authority tends to develop into patrimonialism.

It is unsafe to refer to the Spanish American colonial system as a form of patrimonial domination. For one thing, it is manifestly evident that all forms of Weberian domination existed side by side in the Spanish imperial system. The term *patrimonialism* conjures up the picture of an all-powerful ruler supported by a band of personal retainers. When the patrimonial leader ceases to be present his administration and bureaucracy are naturally supposed to collapse.

However, the Spanish American bureaucracy was not quite patrimonial. In fact, there was a nonpatrimonial professional bureaucracy in Spanish America, exemplified by such men as Juan Martínez de Rozas and José Santiago Portales in Chile and Mariano Moreno in Argentina. All through the colonies there were bureaucrats, often creoles, who were professionals. These people did not serve three or five years in the colonies and then return to Spain, hopefully the richer, but made their living as administrators of the colonial governments at all but the very highest level. Actually, it is difficult to find a region in Spanish America outside a war zone where the bureaucracy failed to function in an orderly fashion and where the administration of government fell apart during the independence movement. In war zones, where economies were disrupted and lines of communication were down, there certainly was often a lack of orderly government. But this was not the fault of a patrimonial bureaucracy unable to function effectively without its traditional head. What is remarkable is how effectively the colonial bureaucracy did function, how in fact it merely went on about its business very much as if there had been no change of government.

Chile has been singled out to support the patrimonial theory. Supposedly Chile's unusual political stability after 1829 was due to the reestablishment of a patrimonial system. Actually, that stability was due to many factors, such as the nature of the economy and society. One of the critical factors in this stability was not the establishment of a patrimonial system of government but rather the establishment of a system of government that was, for its time, remarkably rational-legal. This was the system that Diego Portales desired and attempted to implement. In the legal system it is the impersonal order and the rule of law that reign supreme. The bureaucracy functions within the context of the rule of law, and it owes its allegiance to the legally established impersonal order. Chile shall be discussed in a later chapter. Suffice it to note now that if indeed some form of legal order was established in Chile after 1829, what were its sources? The roots of the legal system were quite alive in the colonial period. Where the soil and topography were appropriate, as in Chile, those roots gained prominence; where they were not, as in Paraguay, patrimonial dictates arose.

Finally, to understand why some colonies became successful nations and others did not we must consider a multitude of factors. We need to take into consideration the geography, the economy, the nature of the society in general, the degree to which the bourgeoisie had matured and formed an integrated oligarchy, the degree to which foreigners controlled economics and politics, the kind of Weberian system—patrimonial or legal—that was established and adhered to, and so on. General theories, Marxist and non-Marxist, as yet have a tendency to obscure rather than illuminate when relied on too heavily.

Notes

1. Quoted in Arthur P. Whitaker, "Enlightenment and Spanish American Independence," in *El Movimiento emancipador de Hispanoamerica,* 4 vols. (Caracas, 1961), 4:55-67.

2. Quoted in David Brading, *Miners and Merchants in Bourbon Mexico, 1763-1810* (Cambridge, 1971), p. 233.

3. Max Weber, *The Theory of Social and Economic Organization* (New York, 1964), p. 341.

CHAPTER THREE

The First Phase of the Independence Movement

The Spanish colonies in America refused to recognize the authority of Joseph Bonaparte; instead, they continued to function more or less as they always had but now in the name of the deposed King Ferdinand VII. The imperial bureaucracy was intact, and a surface calm prevailed generally. But the Spanish crown had been disgraced and Spain itself was in turmoil. During the two years following the accession of Bonaparte there were several ominous signs of the future independence movement.

For instance, on September 16, 1808, a group of peninsulars imprisoned the viceroy of Mexico because of his friendly attitude toward creoles and shipped him off to Spain. The Seville junta then replaced him with another viceroy more appealing to the European Spaniards in Mexico. This was not only a considerable affront to the Mexican creoles, it clearly suggested just how easily a viceroy could be deposed. The capstone of the colonial system was neither inviolate nor permanent. Peninsulars controlled Mexico City until 1821, but the lesson of their actions surely was not lost on creoles throughout the colonies.

Even prior to the Mexican events a viceroy in Spanish America had been ousted by popular will. This occurred in the viceroyalty of the Río de la Plata. In 1806 a British force under the command of Admiral Home Popham and General William Carr Beresford invaded the viceroyalty and captured Buenos Aires. Popham and Beresford had acted under their own orders and not their government's, although they understood that the British government desired to promote the independence of Spanish America, since Spain was an ally of Napoleon. The British governed Buenos Aires temperately, but many *porteños* (residents of the port) left the city and joined an army being formed by Santiago de Liniers, a French sailor who served Spain. Viceroy Sobremonte, who had fled the city, was also gathering an army; but before he could get it under way, Liniers, joined by the residents of Buenos Aires, took the capital and forced the British to sail away. The foreigners had been able to hold Buenos Aires only six weeks.

Later in the year another British force under the command of General John Whitelock invaded and captured Montevideo. Viceroy Sobremonte happened to be there, and again he fled. The *cabildo* of Buenos Aires now deposed the viceroy and gave his military responsibilities to Liniers. Buenos Aires was fast becoming a focal point of patriotic zeal in the colonies. During the summer of 1807 Whitelock crossed the Plate estuary and tried to take Buenos Aires. Liniers and his *porteño* troops were waiting for him, and they drove the British off. The empire was overjoyed and pleased with the *porteños.* Charles IV reacted by proclaiming Liniers interim viceroy. It was a popular choice.

That some Spanish American colonists could both defeat the forces of a major foreign power and depose a viceroy were lessons not lost upon many of the others. And these lessons occurred just as Napoleon's machinations were to humiliate the Spanish monarchy and cut the colonies adrift.

The First Revolts

A year after Joseph Bonaparte became king four revolts racked the colonies. The first centered at the famous University of Chuquisaca in Upper Peru. In May 1809 a junta representing the university and local governing agencies was formed after the example of those in Spain to rule in the name of the deposed king. Chuquisaca now became one of the more radical political centers in the world. In July the *cabildo* of La Paz, which was also in Upper Peru, declared itself the governing authority in its area. In a matter of months both Chuquisaca and La Paz had refused to recognize the authority of the Seville junta. Both rebellions were put down in short order by viceregal forces.

In August a group of creoles caused the *cabildo* of Quito to establish a junta in the name of Ferdinand. This rebellion also was quickly quelled by viceregal forces. Shortly, a similar one took place in Bogotá. It too failed. In December 1809 creoles plotted at Valladolid, Mexico, to overthrow the viceregal administration and to convene a congress of delegates from the leading urban centers to govern in the name of the deposed king. The plot was uncovered before it was put into effect, and several of the conspirators were punished. However, not all of them were caught. There is a direct link between this plot and the famous Hidalgo revolt the following year.

They failed, these 1809 rebellions and plots, but they must have been very inspiring to many creoles who already were questioning the legality of the Seville junta and itching for one of their own.

The 1810 Revolts

There were five major revolts in the Spanish American colonies during 1810, and all of them failed except the one at Buenos Aires. Yet they led eventually to the independence of most of the colonies.

Venezuela

In April 1810 news began reaching the colonies that the patriotic war effort in Spain had failed, that Seville had fallen and the *suprema* was in flight. Many colonists, creoles and peninsulars alike, now thought it was time to establish their own juntas to carry on in Ferdinand's name. In April the *cabildo* of Caracas forced the creation of a junta to govern the capital. It invited other *cabildos* to do the same. Independence from the present government in Spain was soon proclaimed. But the patriot government in Cádiz was more viable than the colonists had thought. It blockaded the Venezuelan coast and sent troops from Cuba. To insure its independence the Caracas government turned to outside help. It concluded that British support would be the factor that might decide the issue. To secure this help a delegation headed by Simón Bolívar was sent to London. Bolívar, the orphan son of a prominent and aristocratic family, who as a youth had been treated to a Rousseauian education, was now twenty-seven years old. He had completed his education in Spain and had traveled to revolutionary France. At eighteen he married a creole in Spain, and in 1802 they returned to Venezuela. He was extraordinarily wealthy and happy, but soon his young wife died. Although never wanting for paramours, he did not marry again. He returned to Europe for several years, where he cultivated radical sentiments.

Probably Bolívar was sent to London in 1810 because his views were somewhat unsettling to many Venezuelans, and this was one way of getting rid of him for a while at least. In dealing with the British government Bolívar faced the same disheartening barriers that would greet diplomats from other colonies for at least a decade. Britain was primarily concerned with the defeat of Napoleon and valued Spain as an ally in the fight. It wanted the empire intact. After Napoleon was defeated and Ferdinand restored, Britain maintained its alliance with Spain. It wanted to trade with the colonies but was not yet willing to disrupt relations with Spain by encouraging an independence movement. Thus Bolívar was not recognized as a visiting diplomat, and his mission to secure British support was a failure—that is, a failure for Venezuela but not for Great Britain. In fear that Britain would support the rebels, the Council of Regency in Cádiz sought to buy off the British by permitting them to trade directly with the colonies for the duration of the war.

Bolívar's instructions permitted him to see the old Venezuelan revolutionary Francisco Miranda, now resident in London after a fascinating and colorful career. Bolívar was very much impressed with Miranda and went as far as to order him to return to Venezuela. On his own account Bolívar envisioned Miranda as the man to lead the independence movement at home.

By the time Bolívar and Miranda arrived in Venezuela late in 1810 the congress that had convened in Caracas to govern the colony had effective control over only a part of the provincial area. Miranda soon became the dominant figure in Caracas. A secret lodge modeled after the one Miranda had established in London was created to guide the independence movement. The degree to which the parent lodge and the subsequent American daughter lodges were Masonic in orientation is subject to speculation, but it is indisputable that the ideals and goals of European free masonry inspired many of the lodge members in the colonies. The lodge, with Miranda and Bolívar in it, quickly seized the initiative and took control of the independence movement in Caracas; on July 5, 1811, the congress declared the independence of republican Venezuela. Venezuela thus became the first Spanish American colony to declare independence, although the congress in Caracas clearly did not speak for the entire colony.

But the first republic endured only one year. Spanish forces under Monteverde, with the support of such Venezuelan elements as the *llaneros*—the mixed-blood cowboys of the Orinoco plains who had little liking for urban civilization—defeated Miranda and his separatist forces. By then Miranda had been granted dictatorial powers by the congress. As a result of the defeat Spanish rule was restored. Miranda was sent back to Spain a prisoner, and he died there a few years later; Bolívar managed to escape to New Granada.

New Granada

The collapse of the Seville junta shocked many creoles and peninsulars alike into action in other regions, and the news of the first successes in Caracas steeled their nerve. The first New Granadan city to create its own junta to rule in the name of Ferdinand was Cartagena, in May 1810. Others followed suit, until, in July 1810, the *cabildo* of the viceregal capital, Santa Fe de Bogotá, did likewise, and in the process deposed the viceroy. The Bogotá junta called a congress to govern the old viceroyalty; but, even more so than in neighboring Venezuela, geographical divisions and cultural and economic differences undermined the chances for unanimity and central government. Some critical regions remained blasé about the coming congress; others were overtly royalist, that is, nonseparatist. Cartagena, which started the process, declared its own independence in 1811. By the time Bolívar and the other Venezuelan refugees arrived in 1812 separatist New Granada was comprised of a Confederation of New Granada, located at Tunja and presided over by Camilo Torres; the independent Cartagena; and the state of Cundinamarca with its capital of Bogotá and its president Antonio Nariño, one of the precursors of Spanish American independence.

Bolívar was not yet thirty when he arrived in the former viceroyalty of New Granada. The confederation made him an officer in its army, and in short order he worked his way up to the rank of brigadier. While fighting royalists and preparing defenses against an invasion from royalist Venezuela he was planning a return home. In May 1813 he took a small army into the Venezuelan mountains and worked his way toward the capital. He was so successful in attracting support that he announced a war to the death against the royalists, something that has embarrassed many of his later admirers. In August 1813 he entered Caracas triumphantly. His determination, his considerable military skill, and his showmanship earned him the title of El Libertador.

The second Venezuelan republic was proclaimed, although this one also could speak for only a part of the former colony. The first one was federalist in orientation, the second centralist, with Bolívar enjoying more or less dictatorial powers. But the Spanish forces under Monteverde had not actually been defeated by Bolívar, and while the second republic was gaining its stride the royalist forces were receiving supplies from Cuba and Puerto Rico. Monteverde's allies were again the *llaneros*, led by José Tomás Boves, who well exemplified the savageness of his followers. In May 1814 Ferdinand was reinstated as king and he proclaimed the restoration of royal absolutism. Thus one could no longer justify an independent government in his name. Many separatists now joined the royalist side. It was only a matter of months until the second republic fell and Bolívar was again in flight.

By the time Bolívar returned to New Granada the situation there had deteriorated markedly. Nariño had been captured and sent to Spain. Bolívar was well received by the confederation and was given the task of subduing Cundinamarca and bringing it into the confederation. This he did with little difficulty, and for his trouble he became captain general of New Granada. He tried to defeat Cartagena also, but there he failed, only preparing it for subsequent royalist conquest. In 1815 Camilo Torres became president of a much enlarged confederation, with its capital now at Bogotá. But the enlarged state did not appear to be in a better position to fight both royalist forces and sentiment. In that year Bolívar gave up the cause and sailed for voluntary exile in Jamaica. At about the same time a major Spanish force of over ten thousand troops under the command of Pablo Morillo landed in Venezuela. Morillo soon took part of the troops to New Granada, where he conquered the port of Cartagena after a siege of several months. Then he took his army up the Magdalena River to meet other troops that had crossed the Andes. In May 1816 he entered Bogotá and put a temporary end to the independence movement in New Granada. The viceregal system was reestablished.

Buenos Aires

Buenos Aires was a commercial town that not only desired complete freedom of choice and action in matters of trade, as did Cartagena, but was confident of its own capabilities when news reached the port of the collapse of the Seville junta. Leaders such as Mariano Moreno and members of the *cabildo* of Buenos Aires pressured the recently arrived viceroy into permitting a general congress to deal with the situation presented by the Spanish events. On May 25 a junta was proclaimed to rule in the name of Ferdinand. The viceroy and other officials were deported.

For basically economic reasons the competing commercial port of Montevideo had traditionally taken positions opposing those of Buenos Aires. Now war broke out between the two rivals, ending in 1814 when Montevideo was captured by the *porteños*. The colony of Paraguay, with its capital of Asunción, was also traditionally fearful of Buenos Aires, and now it too refused to follow the *porteño* lead. An army under the command of Manuel Belgrano was sent from Buenos Aires to subdue Asunción, but at this it failed. However, shortly an independent state was established in Paraguay, one that the *porteños* never managed to incorporate into their political-commercial system.

If Montevideo and Asunción were important to Buenos Aires, then Upper Peru, which later became Bolivia, was supremely so. Asunción meant trade, and Montevideo controlled the entrance to the Plate estuary, but Upper Peru meant silver and a major market for Argentine products and transshipped European goods. Upper Peru was also strategically important in the Argentine desire to separate Peru itself from the empire. Thus an expeditionary force was sent to Upper Peru, but in 1811 it was defeated.

A year after the junta was established in Buenos Aires it was clear that only a minor portion of the former viceroyalty of the Río de la Plata had fallen under the suzerainty of Buenos Aires. Buenos Aires itself was flourishing under the new system; but many provincial towns suffered, especially those that were accustomed to trading with Upper Peru, whose market was now closed to them by the royalists. The basis of a federalist-centralist conflict was already outlined.

In 1811 political power in Buenos Aires was centered in an executive triumverate, an experiment that lasted three years. A congress convened in 1813 was supposedly representative of the United Provinces of the Río de la Plata, but actually it was representative of only a portion of the former viceroyalty. In 1814 the triumvirate was superseded by a supreme director. With independence movements falling to the wayside all around them the *porteños* understood that to consolidate their position they must enlist the support of other provinces. In 1816 another congress was convened, this time at Tucumán, rather than Buenos Aires. The deputies considered many and somewhat conflicting paths to follow. Finally they decided to declare unequivocal independence from Spain. A new supreme director, Juan Martín Pueyrredón, a man of commanding administrative talent, was elected. He governed for three years.

In the meantime events were not going well in Montevideo, capital of the region called the Banda Oriental, the eastern shore of the River Uruguay. From the interior José Gervasio Artigas had led a force of gauchos into Montevideo to defeat the *porteños* and drive them out. Artigas established a federalist confederation, including several important Argentine provinces. In 1816, however, the Brazilians attacked the Banda Oriental and the following year took Montevideo. The Banda Oriental was annexed by Brazil, and Artigas went into exile in Paraguay.

Chile

By the time news reached Chile of the dismal events in Spain the captain general had alienated so many people that the *audiencia* feared outright rebellion. Consequently it requested that the captain general resign. This he did on July 16, 1810. The position devolved by law upon Brigadier Mateo de Toro Zambrano, Conde de la Conquista. Born in Santiago and well over eighty years old, Toro Zambrano was one of Chile's most prominent landowners, one who had been a highly successful merchant. His promotion to the rank of brigadier only the year before was no doubt inspired by a desire to secure his allegiance. He seemed an excellent choice for captain general. Not only was he the highest ranking military official in Chile, but he was held in great esteem by his fellows and he was a Chilean. However, the tense situation proved to be more than he could handle.

Less than two months after he became captain general, the situation had deteriorated to such a point that Toro Zambrano feared open warfare. To avert an internecine conflict he called for a *cabildo abierto* to meet on September 18. Several hundred people attended and voted for the creation of a national junta. It was licensed as only a provisional body, to function until a national assembly could convene.

It is often said that the first Spanish American juntas were radical bodies and represented the triumph of creole over peninsular. The composition of the Chilean junta suggests that this generalization must be viewed cautiously. The *cabildo abierto* elected Toro Zambrano president of the junta. For vice-president, José Antonio Martínez, bishop-elect of Santiago, was selected. The body of the junta was supposed to comprise three *vocales*. First *vocal* was Fernando Márquez de la Plata, born in Spain to a distinguished family and in his own right a leading government official. Juan Martínez de Rozas was elected second *vocal*. For third *vocal* the *cabildo abierto* chose Ignacio de la Carrera, a prominent landowner from Santiago. No plans were made for additional members, but the general sentiment favored the election of two more *vocales*. Consequently, over four hundred people voted a second time during the same *cabildo abierto* and elected Francisco Javier Reina and Juan Enrique Rosales. The former was a colonel of artillery and a fervent supporter of the old regime. The latter was elected to represent the powerful Larraín family (to which he belonged by marriage), whose enormous size and influence permitted it to be in itself a political grouping called the *ochocientos*.

One could hardly consider the junta a radical body. Pains were taken to assure both the Council of Regency and Ferdinand that a very respectable movement was under way. Only the views of Rozas might be held suspect; but he was elected, in part at least, to insure the loyalty of Concepción. It is true that several leading Chileans considered the establishment of the junta more than just an unusual event; they perceived in it a major indication that independence could be a reality in the near future. But the overwhelming majority of the active citizenry saw in the junta either a means of preserving the empire intact under pressure for reform or a means of achieving reform without destroying the empire, which, though distinctly different points of view, amounted to the same thing. It was only during the immediate years after 1810 that a potent, popular sentiment developed in support of independence; and only after independence was declared did it become stylish to refer to September 18, 1810, as the first step toward it. The same was probably true in other colonies. Chile began to govern itself in 1810 and for this privilege fought a war with the viceroyalty of Peru in 1813. It was during these three years that Chileans cultivated an avid predilection for self-government.

On December 15 the junta called for the meeting of a national congress. The convocation decree stated that representatives of the entire realm were to meet in Santiago to decide upon the system that best suited its "regimen security and prosperity during the absence of the king." It met the following year and elected a new junta, one whose powers were pointedly subject to congressional control. However, in September 1811 José Miguel Carrera seized control of the congress. Born in Santiago in 1786, he had only arrived back home from a study trip to Spain at the end of July. Yet before he was twenty-six he controlled the government of Chile. Several factors contributed to this. Carrera's father, Ignacio de la Carrera, was descended from the early conquistadors and was a member of one of the colony's most aristocratic families. His brothers were military officers in control of key forces. Perhaps most important, by the end of August there was no other dynamic personality in Santiago to lead Chile out of the calm which had fallen on the colony.

But at once other juntas sprang up to represent local interests. The most important was the one established in Concepción. However, while the provinces and the capital were in the process of invoking a final confrontation, the Carrera-inspired congress proceeded to produce a commendable record and become the center of progressive activity in Chile. Soon the Carreras seized even more power in the capital, and the south of Chile prepared its forces for war. At this point an invasion force sent by the viceroy of Peru landed in the south, and both provinces joined in the fight to preserve the Chilean homeland. The Peruvians arrived in March 1813 and finally defeated the Chileans in October 1814. For the next three years Chile was again controlled by the Peruvian viceregal administration.

Mexico

No event of the Spanish American independence movement has captured the fancy of later generations more than Hidalgo's ringing of the bell in his parish church at Dolores on September 16, 1810–calling hundreds, then thousands and scores of thousands of Indians to fight behind the standard of the Virgin of Guadalupe and in the name of Ferdinand for a government that would treat them more equitably. Father Miguel Hidalgo y Costilla was a creole who was well known to the church for his liberal views; in fact he had even been investigated by the Inquisition. Among his more radical activities (not to mention for the moment his plot of rebellion), he encouraged his Indian parishioners to pursue economic activities such as viniculture and light manufactures, something at odds with administrative policy.

Hidalgo had been a member of a group of enlightened creoles who conspired at Querétero, in the silver-mining region to the northwest of Mexico City, to oust peninsulars from the viceregal government. A multiple uprising was envisioned, but authorities learned of the plan before it could be consummated. With little time to spare, Hidalgo made his famous *grito*, his call at Dolores that started the rebellion. Probably he did not speak to the Indians at length about independence or protecting the homeland against possible invasion, something he and his fellow conspirators thought about considerably, since the Indians were not much concerned about such matters. But they had their grievances, familiar to Indians throughout the colonies, and these had been brought into sharper focus by agricultural crises and the rising cost of corn during the last decades of the colonial period.

Hidalgo was joined at first by some leading creoles, but soon the bitterness and savageness he had loosed upon the Mexican countryside scared many off. It even frightened Hidalgo, who had not imagined that a race war would develop from his more limited plans. Tens of thousands of Indians left the fields and mines, joined Hidalgo's armies, and satisfied a rage that had been building over the centuries. Not only were many people killed, but the damage to property was profound—haciendas were destroyed, and mines without Indians to work them filled with water—and would challenge Mexico's best intentions for some time to come.

In January 1811 Hidalgo was defeated by Spanish and creole forces. In March he was captured, and in July he was executed. The movement was taken over by another parish priest, José María Morelos, a man of greater military and administrative ability. Morelos was less of an intellectual than Hidalgo and, fortunately for the revolution he headed, emphatically more pragmatic. He gave his followers a more specific program than had Hidalgo, emphasizing social and racial equality, complete independence from Spain, and the perpetuation of the Catholic religion. Morelos attracted intellectuals to the fold, and in 1813 a congress convened and the constitution of Apatzingán was written. He continued the war that had started at Dolores until 1815, when he was captured and executed. This appeared to be the end of the Mexican independence movement. During the next few years patriot guerrilla forces continued to operate in isolated regions, but the colony as a whole was governed by the traditional viceregal administration as it slowly recovered from the economic dislocations of the war.

By the end of 1816 all the independence movements in Spanish America, except the one at Buenos Aires, had been effectively stifled. Additionally, the powerful and strategic viceroyalty of Peru had not even taken the first steps toward independence. Nor had the Central American colonies or Cuba and Puerto Rico. Not many people would have thought that the independence movement would get under way again in 1817, this time successfully.

CHAPTER FOUR

The Second Phase of the Independence Movement

Two men loom largest and practically overwhelm all others during the successful phase of the independence movement. Both operated in South America–Bolívar in the north and José de San Martín in the south–and both reignited the movement in 1817. Ferdinand was back on the throne of Spain, so no one could properly speak of independence in his name. Now it was all or nothing; now the king of Spain could ostracize rebels and send troops; now it was a full-fledged independence movement.

San Martín, O'Higgins and the Liberation of Chile

San Martín was born in the viceroyalty of the Río de la Plata in 1778 and sent as a boy to Spain for his education as a soldier. He worked his way up the ranks to the position of lieutenant colonel, but in 1811 he deserted the Spanish army and fled to England. In London he was inducted into Miranda's secret lodge. It was there certainly that any thoughts about the independence of his homeland were nurtured. He arrived at Buenos Aires in 1812, in time to take part in the independence movement there, actively organizing military forces. Eventually he left the army for the governorship of Cuyo under the pretext of poor health; but it is quite likely that he believed his continental plan could be brought to fruition more effectively from Cuyo, a province which bordered on and included part of the Andes, than from Buenos Aires. The permanent independence of the United Provinces, San Martín was convinced, could be insured only by the liberation of the rest of the continent. This meant that the powerful and prestigious viceroyalty of Peru must be liberated sooner or later. There were several ways of approaching Peru, but San Martín came to believe that it would be best to secure the freedom of Chile first.

This suited the interests of the many Chilean refugees, including Bernardo O'Higgins, who had fled across the Andes in 1814 and had spent the next three years in Argentina planning or thinking about the liberation of their homeland. In early January 1817 San Martín mobilized his combined Army of the Andes, a force that included Chileans, and headed across the Andes in one of the most spectacular feats in the history of military logistics. The royalists were taken by surprise, and on February 12, 1817, they met the invading forces on the plains of Chacabuco, to the northeast of Santiago. San Martín's forces won the battle and quickly entered the capital.

Subsequent events in Santiago are very important for an understanding of the nature of the first Chilean government and of Bernardo O'Higgins's later fall from power. As soon as the royalists fled Santiago the *cabildo* elected an interim governor. On February 15 an assembly of notables elected San Martín governor of Chile and granted him unlimited powers. San Martín refused the position. On the following day the assembly again elected San Martín, and again he refused. It then proceeded at the same session to elect O'Higgins interim supreme director. O'Higgins was the choice both of San Martín and of the government that had sponsored the liberation of Chile. That O'Higgins would become supreme director had been decided long before in Buenos Aires; San Martín's instructions were specific on the matter. O'Higgins himself knew of this decision before crossing the Andes.

But this is exactly as it should have been. It was natural for the Chileans to express their gratitude to San Martín, the man who quite dramatically liberated them. And it was natural for the Argentines to want O'Higgins as head of the new government. Chile, after all, represented merely the first stage in the Argentine plan for the liberation of the South American continent. It was in their interest to keep San Martín free to proceed to Peru and to place a Chilean dedicated to the overall plan in the new directorship. O'Higgins on all accounts was a likely choice. He was the ranking Chilean in the combined army, a close personal friend of San Martín, and a leading Chilean patriot. O'Higgins represented the broad continental plan to the Argentines and nationhood to the Chileans. He became supreme director because of a military feat, not because he had garnered the support of a reasonably large portion of the active citizenry, or any part of it. Slightly over two hundred government officials and residents of Santiago elected him to the post as their second choice and in the early excitement of victory.

Once independence was declared officially in 1818 and once the element of nationalism became a factor, especially after San Martín departed for Peru in 1820, O'Higgins began to remind Chileans more of their Argentine benefactor than of their own national inviolability. This was the catalyst that activated the resentment of various segments of the population to his specific governmental actions. Alone, this animosity might not have caused his downfall in 1823; but in conjunction with his changed identity, at least as Chileans conceived it, it was too powerful a force to fail in achieving his overthrow.

Although the Chileans still had to fight royalist elements in the south for years, the independence of the new state was effectively secured with the entrance of the Army of the Andes into Santiago. O'Higgins governed, at times more radically than various segments of the society (such as the church and landed rich) desired, until January 1823. The problems of the first Chilean government shall be examined in later chapters. For now one final point must be considered.

Miranda's secret London lodge and its offshoots in the colonies have already been mentioned. A view of the role of the Chilean branch during the O'Higgins years will permit one to gauge the power of these lodges in other new states. The Chilean branch was called the *Logia lautarina.* The impetus for its founding was furnished by San Martín, who was determined to create a branch of the Buenos Aires lodge. It was a secret organization dedicated to the liberation of Spanish America. According to its statutes any brother who revealed its existence would be punished by death. Should a brother become a government official he could not make any important decisions without first consulting the lodge. In an emergency a brother could act as he saw fit, but only under the condition that he would report his actions to the lodge. No brother in government could make any major appointments without lodge approval; and major appointments included those of diplomats, governors of provinces, generals, justices, high ecclesiastical officials, and regimental chiefs of the army or militia. Since no official lodge records exist, we cannot say precisely who belonged; nor can we say what it actually accomplished. It is certain that San Martín and O'Higgins belonged and that between February 1817 and the sailing of the expedition to Peru in August 1820 the lodge was the power which governed Chile. Once San Martín and his *Expedición Libertadora* finally left Chile for Peru, the lodge no longer could justify its existence. And in fact, in terms of influence, it ceased to exist just at that moment. Then O'Higgins began to remind Chileans of the foreign origins of their independence and government more intensely than before—something they preferred to forget.

It is not likely that the Spanish American lodges generally reached such power and influence as those in Argentina, Chile, and Peru. This was in part because San Martín was an organization man while Bolívar was more flamboyant, something of a one-man institution of government in himself. Probably Bolívar would not have tolerated what San Martín would have encouraged. Yet there were lodges in the Bolivarian lands, and they often had considerable influence. The independence movement in general thus had its revolutionary cadre, its party. It must be given credit for the consummation of independence. One would like to know how situations might have differed if the lodges had expanded into controlling political parties once independence was achieved.

Peru

In August 1820 San Martín took his *Expedición Libertadora*, comprising several thousand Chileans and Argentines, to Peru by means of a Chilean fleet commanded by one of the most colorful and controversial figures of the entire Spanish American independence movement, Lord

Thomas Cochrane. Many British citizens distinguished themselves in the independence movement, but none more dramatically than Cochrane. By 1821 San Martín had captured the port of Pisco, to the south of Lima, and Cochrane was blockading Callao, Lima's port; but so far there was no general uprising in support of the forces of liberation, as San Martín had calculated would occur. Finally, San Martín moved his army to a position north of Lima. Again he expected the Peruvians to share his enthusiasm for liberation and rise up against the viceroy. While his officers—especially some of those not under his direct supervision, like Cochrane—grew restless through the lack of resolution and action, San Martín entered into fruitless negotiations with Viceroy Joaquín de Pezuela. Both seemed determined to avoid an ultimate confrontation. Eventually, San Martín elected to march toward Lima, and, as he approached, the royalist army deposed Pezuela and selected a new viceroy. Owing to Lima's low food supply (rather than to military weakness) the new viceroy shortly withdrew. On July 10, 1821, the army of the *Expedición Libertadora* entered Lima in passive triumph.

The independence of Peru was quickly proclaimed, and San Martín became the chief of state, with the title *Protector.* But the new government did not control all of Peru; a powerful royalist army still roamed the countryside with little interference. San Martín himself did not take easily to the transition from soldier to statesman. He was beset by a multitude of problems that quite vexed him. Adding to the many perplexing daily problems of domestic government was the burdensome issue of how to continue the momentum of the independence movement itself. By now Bolívar was having great successes in northern South America. In 1822 he invited San Martín to the port of Guayaquil in Ecuador to discuss the liberation of royalist Peru. They met, the two preeminent generals of the independence movement, in July of that year. It is not clear what was said at the meeting. It is certain, however, that San Martín's inclination toward monarchism could not have sat well with Bolívar's autocratic republicanism and that Bolívar had momentum on his side; San Martín had clearly lost his. The Argentine was also troubled by the problems his government was facing in Lima and by his poor health. After meeing with Bolívar, San Martín decided to withdraw to Lima and permit Bolívar to lead the independence movement in the rest of Peru. He returned to Lima to find that his most influential minister, Monteagudo, had been expelled from office, a popularly acclaimed event. San Martín did not attempt to reestablish his authority; instead he sailed for Chile and then went to Argentina. Shortly thereafter he left for permanent self-imposed exile in Europe. Bolívar was now free to continue the independence movement in Peru.

Bolívar in the North

The same year that San Martín took his Army of the Andes into Chile, 1817, Bolívar began the long process of organizing a liberation movement in the north. The year before with Haitian support, in return for which he promised to free the slaves in South America, Bolívar had undertaken an unsuccessful filibustering expedition to Venezuela. Now in 1817 he landed at the mouth of the Orinoco River and worked his way into the interior. There he came into contact with various guerrilla and renegade paramilitary groups. Now relying on the appeal of his aristocratic bearing, now employing tactics that would have done the most uncivilized of the renegade chieftains proud, Bolívar managed to establish his authority and leadership over the various factions. Most important, he won the support of José Antonio Páez, the young leader of a powerful force of *llaneros*. During the first phase of the independence movement the separatists had been defeated by the royalists in part because the *llaneros*, under Boves, fought against them. Now Bolívar had them on his side. It was a major achievement.

Bolívar stayed at Angostura on the lower Orinoco for about two years, during which time he received matériel from British merchants and was joined by many British soldiers and citizens. With a force of several thousand men, including about five hundred formerly British troops, Bolívar started the campaign that in half a dozen years would liberate extensive territories and cause the creation of five new states. Using Páez and his *llaneros* and Francisco de Paula Santander with other troops in diversionary tactics, Bolívar took his main force over the Andes to the plains of New Granada. There at Boyacá he easily defeated the defending royalist forces in August 1819. With no trouble at all he entered Bogotá and liberated the capital of the viceroyalty. Bolívar quickly departed for his base of operations on the Orinoco, leaving Santander, only twenty-seven at the time, in charge of the government of the former viceroyalty. Yet major portions of New Granada were still securely under royalist control.

Under pressure from the triumphant Bolívar, a congress at Angostura created a new republic called Colombia, comprising the liberated portions of New Granada and Venezuela. Bolívar was named the country's first president, and at once he set out on a new expedition. At this juncture events in Spain again resounded forcefully in the New World and threatened the very existence of the empire. For some time Ferdinand VII had been gathering a giant military expedition at Cádiz, at times reaching more than twenty thousand troops, with which he expected to reestablish his authority in the former colonies. The arrival of an army of such size might well have turned the tide against the new states. Spanish America at the end of 1819 was still only partly independent; many large and strategic areas remained royalist. And the major foreign powers were not yet prepared to support the colonists directly. Kings were not anxious to see one of their coreligionists humiliated and stripped of valuable territories by his subjects. This was the era of the Congress of Vienna and the Holy Alliance. Even the United States was not prepared to jeopardize its interests, especially the diplomatic acquisition of Florida from Spain. Seeing the troops at Cádiz, not many people would have wagered against Ferdinand at the end of 1819.

On the first day of January 1820 a regiment of the troops gathered at Cádiz rebelled and proclaimed the restoration of the defunct liberal constitution of 1812. Some troops had been at Cádiz for several years and had become demoralized. Secret lodges, often with liberal political inclinations, had sprung up within the army to promote rebellion against the king. The revolt, led by Colonel Rafael Riego, now found fertile ground throughout Spain, and other units joined the movement. With the defection of the Madrid forces Ferdinand realized that a concerted fight against the movement now might lead to his deposition. Thus in March 1820 Ferdinand seized the moment and placed himself at the head of the liberal movement by proclaiming the restoration of the 1812 constitution and calling for the convocation of the *Cortes*. But the new liberal Spain did not satisfy the Spanish American liberals or conservatives. The independence movement continued, but now without the threat of a major military invasion from Europe.

Once San Martín departed from Peru the Peruvians attempted to govern themselves and continue their own independence movement. They did not seem anxious to have Bolívar around. However, within a year the situation had deteriorated to such an extent that in May 1823 the Peruvian congress requested Bolívar's support. Bolívar responded by sending a few thousand troops under the command of Antonio José Sucre, a young Venezuelan who had just defeated the Spanish forces at the battle of Pichincha, outside Quito, in May 1822, thus creating the state of Ecuador, a part of Bolívar's Colombia. Bolívar himself did not arrive in Peru until September 1823.

Just at this time events in the Iberian peninsula again threatened the independence of Spanish America. In 1823 the Holy Alliance decided to deal with the Spanish liberal revolution through military intervention. Great Britain did not support the venture, but neither did it oppose it forcibly. A massive French army invaded Spain and this time was not repulsed by the Spaniards. By autumn 1823 royal absolutism had been established once more. A liberal movement in Portugal was also overturned, and royal absolutism was proclaimed there too. Britain and the United States were both concerned that now the independence movement in the New World would be thwarted and the lucrative new markets closed to international trade. Britain encouraged the United States to join in a combined declaration against European intervention in the New World. In the process Britain issued the strategically important secret Polignac Memorandum, which quite effectively protected the new states. Before a joint statement could be worked out, President James Monroe made his famous declaration of December 1823 against foreign intervention in the New World that has come to be known as the Monroe Doctrine. Spanish Americans well understood that it was not the Monroe message that protected them but the British navy. Nevertheless, the independence movement was permitted to proceed.

Bolívar waited until well into 1824 before meeting the main royalist forces in Peru. They met in August near Lake Junín, high in the Andes. The patriots won the day, and the royalists retired to Cuzco. The Spanish forces, including thousands of Peruvians, made their final stand at Ayacucho, midway between Cuzco and Lima, in December 1824. The patriot army, led by Sucre, was outnumbered, but it defeated the royalists. Although there were mopping-up operations to be undertaken, the battle of Ayacucho effectively ended Spanish military opposition to the Spanish American independence movement.

Mexico

Mexico did not become involved in the second phase of the independence movement until quite late. The Hidalgo-Morelos revolution had caused serious disruption; but during the five years after Morelos's death the colony had regained its stride, and the viceregal administration was secure and confident. Ferdinand's proclamation of the liberal constitution of 1812 and his summoning of a new *Cortes* in 1820 undermined all this. The viceroy was constrained to lessen the restraints of the colonial government, and a liberal approach was everywhere the order of the day. But the new Mexican and Spanish liberalism only fired the desires of the Mexican liberals and scandalized the conservatives, especially members of the upper clergy. For quite opposite reasons both liberals and conservatives in Mexico began thinking about independence in complete seriousness.

The man who took advantage of this situation and led Mexico to independence was Agustín de Iturbide. Iturbide was born in 1783 in Western Mexico to a prominent landowning family. During the first phase of the independence movement he fought with the royalist forces against the patriots. In reward for his military successes, Colonel Iturbide was made military commander of a district comprising the provinces of Guanajuato and Michoacán in 1815. The harshness and irregularities of his rule led to serious discontent among the citizens of his district. They managed to secure his recall in 1816. Not enough evidence could be collected against Iturbide, and instead of being dismissed from the army he was relieved of his command and placed in a sort of military limbo. As late as 1820 there were still a few insurgent bands of guerrillas roaming the Mexican countryside. Attempts to quash them did not go well, and in 1820 the viceroy decided that Iturbide might be the man to do the job. In November 1820 Colonel Iturbide accepted the appointment of commander of the royalist forces charged with dealing with the insurgent bands, and that month he marched against the most important rebel leader, Vicente Guerrero.

Instead of fighting the rebel leader, Iturbide made a deal with him. They agreed to join forces, and in February 1821 they issued the joint *Plan de Iguala*. The *plan* was entirely pragmatic, appealing to just about everyone in the colony. It declared the independence of Mexico from Spain and embodied three basic principles. One was that the new government should be a monarchy, preferably headed by Ferdinand himself or a member of his family or someone from another royal house. Another was that the Roman Catholic religion would continue its traditional position and be the only one tolerated in the new country. The third established the principle of racial equality. However, the colored castes thought this meant equality between them and the whites, while the whites thought this meant equality between creoles and peninsulars. Nevertheless, the three principles together won a broad spectrum of support throughout the colony. An Army of the Three Guarantees was created to carry out the *plan*.

Mexico also had its conspiracy of secret lodges to which many military men belonged. They supported the new movement, and one after another garrison joined the rebels. News of rebel successes bestirred soldiers in the capital itself, and finally the military officialdom pressured the viceroy to resign. This he did in early July. Even before Viceroy Juan Ruíz de Apodaca resigned, the liberal Spanish *Cortes* had appointed General Juan O'Donojú to replace him. O'Donjú arrived at Veracruz in August 1821 to find his viceroyalty in a political shambles.

The new viceroy was determined to govern with the support of the Mexican population. Late in the same month that he arrived in Mexico O'Donojú met with Iturbide in the town of Córdoba. The two of them signed a treaty named for the town in which their meeting took place. It confirmed, with modest alterations, the *Plan de Iguala*. Thus Mexican independence had been agreed to by the leading Spanish official in the realm. Toward the end of September 1821 Iturbide marched into Mexico City. A junta, including O'Donojú, was soon selected, and it elected Iturbide its first president. A declaration of independence was issued forthwith.

The governing junta soon appointed a regency to act as the executive branch of government until an emperor might be chosen. When Iturbide became president of the regency he resigned his position as president of the junta. In February of the following year a congress met to supersede the junta as the legislative body. According to the *Plan de Iguala* and the Treaty of Córdoba, the new Mexican government would offer a crown to Ferdinand, to a member of his family if he declined, or to some other royal prince. Before a terribly exhaustive search could be made, a street crowd proclaimed Iturbide the new emperor. The following day, May 20, 1822, the congress did likewise, and on May 21

Iturbide became Emperor Agustín I. Several provinces that were not physically part of the old viceroyalty–including the captaincy general of Guatemala (Central America)–soon joined the new Mexican empire.

Opposition to the new emperor was quick in developing. A major rebellion against him, led by Antonio López de Santa Anna and Guadalupe Victoria (two future presidents of Mexico), began even before the end of 1822. In March 1823 Agustín resigned, and in May he went into exile. The empire was dissolved and a republican form of government established.

Central America

Central America became independent through the gravitational pull of the successful Mexican movement. Today Central America comprises the tropical nations of Guatemala, El Salvador, Honduras, Nicaragua, and Costa Rica. During the colonial period the five provinces belonged theoretically to the viceroyalty of New Spain (Mexico), but in practice they were governed by the captain general and *audiencia* of Guatemala. The independence movement itself was led by the captain general, the Spanish General Gabino Gainza. It was proclaimed on September 15, 1821. In January 1822 Central America became part of the Mexican empire. With the fall of Iturbide and the empire the Central American states merely went on about their business and remained independent.

Actually it was not quite so simple. Central America was plagued by political problems, but fundamentally these revolved around the federalist-centralist debate that was so prevalent in Spanish America. (This debate will be considered in the following chapters.)

Other Regions

By the middle of the 1820s Argentina, Mexico, Venezuela, New Granada (later to be called Colombia), Ecuador, Bolivia, Peru, Chile, Central America, and Paraguay were independent. Little has been said about Paraguay. It was one of the most isolated and backward of the Spanish colonies. It managed to become independent in 1811 and to remain so. From 1814 to 1840 Paraguay was ruled absolutely and unequivocally by José Gaspar Rodríguez de Francia. He was certainly the most successful of the early dictators, and he gave Paraguay an extreme form of stability, one that was arrantly indolent and retarding.

It took Uruguay a little longer than the others to become independent. The Banda Oriental was conquered by Brazil in 1817 and then annexed into the Brazilian empire. In 1825 a small group of Uruguayan refugees crossed over from Buenos Aires and began a rebellion. The *porteños* supported the rebel efforts, and for the next three years Buenos Aires and Brazil were involved in minor conflict over the Banda Oriental. Finally, in 1828 Great Britain forced both to recognize the existence of Uruguay as an independent buffer state separating the two powers.

Santo Domingo remained a colony, but this time a colony of Haiti. In 1822 the Haitians conquered Santo Domingo and kept it in colonial status for the next two decades. Cuba and Puerto Rico did not strike out for independence but merely remained part of the Spanish empire. Brazil became an independent empire in 1822.

Two aspects of the Spanish American independence movement might well be considered within the context of the events of independence. They are the role of the Catholic church and the question of foreign recognition.

The Church and Independence

Generally the lower clergy supported the independence movement and the upper clergy, the hierarchy, remained loyal to Spain. The lower clergy were hit particularly hard by the Bourbon reforms at the end of the colonial period. Curtailment of the privilege of personal immunity in criminal cases aroused not only members of the local clergy but also their local parishioners. Perhaps more important, however, were the economic reforms, particularly the attack on the chantries and pious works. These reforms seriously undercut the modest economic position of the lower clergy, who were often dependent solely on these sources for their meager incomes. Members of the lower clergy were involved in practically all the early schemes for independence. But even many of those who were not political activists got caught up in the momentum of the independence movement once it commenced, and often as they went so too did their flocks.

With the establishment of the liberal government and the new *Cortes* in Spain after Riego's revolt in 1820, the situation changed markedly. The *Cortes* passed laws so radical that they forced important members of the upper clergy to join the independence movement. The liberal government of 1812 had terminated the immunity of insurgent priests. Now in 1820 a permanent law did the same for all priests, even those who had remained loyal to Spain. Monastic orders, not including the mendicant orders, were now suppressed. And other highly radical anti-church laws were enacted. Members of the upper clergy quickly decided that they could better protect their own position and that of the church also by joining and influencing the independence movement and the writing of new constitutions. Thus the upper clergy supported Iturbide, who was careful to guarantee the traditional position of the church. One of the most famous changes of allegiance after the new liberal laws of 1820 and thereafter was made by Bishop Lasso of Mérida. He once wrote that when Ferdinand VII recognized the rebellion of 1820 and swore allegiance to the 1812 liberal constitution, the Spanish Americans regained their sovereignty. Perhaps he was a bit too impressed with the power of the upper clergy, but the support they now gave clearly strengthened the independence movement. Lasso became an ardent supporter of independence and the first bishop to write to the Vatican on behalf of the independence movement.

In addition to the allegiance of both the upper and lower clergy the new nations ardently desired papal recognition. This would have made an invasion highly unlikely and would have encouraged recognition by the major European powers. Two bishops of Colombia, Lasso of Mérida and Jiménez of Popayán, wrote to the pope to induce him to support the independence of Spanish America. Pius VII received the first of the letters, from Lasso, in 1822. The pope answered by assuming a neutral position, which was a great victory for the independence movement. In 1816 the pope had supported the mother country. Several of the new nations sent diplomatic representatives to Rome to secure recognition. But their chances declined significantly in 1824 with the accession of Leo XII to the papal throne. The new pope was confronted with the fact that Ferdinand VII had been restored to his full absolutist powers by the Holy Alliance. In 1824 the pope issued an encyclical that urged the Spanish American hierarchy to support Ferdinand. This was a considerable blow to the Spanish Americans who favored independence. The papacy did not recognize the independence of the new Spanish American nations until after the accession of Gregory XVI in 1831, but by then it was not so valuable an item as it would have been a decade earlier.

Foreign Recognition

Great Britain and the United States had an earnest rivalry over Spanish America. Both wanted to dominate the new and gigantic commercial market represented by the former colonies, but neither was very interested in territorial aggrandizement, although some North Americans had a fancy for certain contiguous lands and even Cuba. The United States could more easily support the independence movement openly since it was not conceptually tied to the Spanish monarchy, as was Great Britain. Yet the United States was restricted by its interest in acquiring Florida and the later negotiations that achieved this. The Spanish Americans thought that recognition by either of these two powers probably would make the independence of Spanish America irrevocable. The new nations concentrated their efforts on Great Britain and sent diplomats there, but these novices were in for tough times in London. The plight of the Chilean representative, José de Irissari, was somewhat typical.

Irisarri arrived in London in 1818 displaying boundless optimism. Since his primary goal was to secure recognition, he set out to impress the London community. He quartered himself well, rode around town in a fine carriage replete with liveried coachmen, and proposed to invite influential people to his residence. All this was designed to suggest that many well-placed people had an interest in the future of Chile. Before the end of 1818 the limited funds that the Chilean government could afford to send him put an end to this grandiose scheme. In 1819 he was relegated to life in a boarding house. Perhaps the knowledge that other Spanish American representatives with similar schemes already had ended up in debtors' prison induced him to take these economies. At any rate, his first diplomatic efforts were not successful. He focused his attention on Lord Castlereagh, hoping to convince the prime minister of the advantageous nature of recognition to all concerned. But he was forced to do this indirectly, since Castlereagh continually refused to meet with the Chilean plenipotentiary, an act which some surely would construe as being tantamount to recognition. But in 1819 the British government decided to maintain a policy of strict neutrality in the Spanish American wars. Now the prime minister could greet the Spanish American representatives officially without offending anyone, and this he did. This was really a form of de facto recognition.

It was the United States that first officially recognized the independence of the Spanish American nations. In March 1822 President Monroe sent a message to Congress in which he recognized the independence of Chile, Argentina, Peru, Colombia, and Mexico. Great Britain did not recognize the independence of the new nations until 1825. Recognition by the United States occurred prior to the final battles of independence, two years before the battle at Ayacucho. Recognition by Great Britain was less bold; it took place after Ayacucho and after the proclamation of Monroe's celebrated "hands off" message of 1823.

With Great Britain's recognition in 1825 the independence of Spanish America was irreversible—at least in the traditional political sense.

CHAPTER FIVE

The Independence Leaders as Liberals

The Spanish American independence movement was not a revolution; it was a civil revolt, although the individual movements at times manifested revolutionary overtones, and the early Mexican movement was clearly revolutionary in direction. Overall, the independence movement was an Americanization of the machinery of government. The shift to republicanism that almost always attended the movement was hardly radical; it was, in fact, quite harmonious with Spanish political theory in the post-1810 period. Although the early constitutions generally abolished slavery, they often incorporated voting qualifications such as the possession of real property or liquid capital. At times, farmhands, domestic employees, and people in debt to the public treasury were eliminated, although not permanently, from the franchise. A great many people were allowed to vote but were not effectively part of the active citizenry. These people were usually so controlled by their employers that their right to vote meant very little. In some fundamental ways the independence movement passed them by.

The movement was carried out by the active citizenry—the oligarchy and those people on the way up from the lower ranges of society. Others fought for independence by generally doing what they were told, with little appreciation for the consequences of their actions. All sectors of society contributed to the personalities of the new nations, but the contribution of the active citizenry has often been misjudged.

By and large the Spanish American independence leaders were liberals, in the nineteenth century sense of the term, and not democrats. They were liberals after Locke and Montesquieu, just as were Jefferson, Madison, and Hamilton. And many of them, like Pueyrredón of Argentina and Bello of Venezuela and Chile, were quite influenced by Bentham's utilitarianism. They were clearly not democrats in the sense of Rousseau's general will, and in fact they wrote constitutions that, like the United States constitution, carefully guarded against the appearance of democracy. There were democrats or men with democratic leanings among them, like Carrera of Chile, just as there were in the United States; but these men were quickly repressed and their ideas pushed aside for nearly half a century. They might invoke the name of Rousseau to justify their rebellions for independence, as did Mariano Moreno of Buenos Aires, but it must be remembered that Rousseau's ideas on kings and the governed strikingly reflected Suárez's views. That is, fundamental elements of Rousseauian philosophy were quite prominent in traditional Spanish political theory. And even so, when Moreno translated and printed the *Social Contract* to justify the Buenos Aires rebellion for independence he did so selectively; he deleted the religious sections that offended him. Moreno wrote: "Since Rousseau had the misfortune to rant and rave when he dealt with religion, I suppressed that chapter and the principal passages in which he has treated these matters."[1]

Moreno and countless other leaders throughout the colonies wanted what they considered freedom of the press. They had lived under an intolerable press censorship, and now with independence they wanted freedom of expression. As classical liberals their concept of freedom of expression was limited, but no doubt within the confines of their own conception of society they thought they were advocating complete freedom of expression. Again Moreno wrote: "At last we perceive that the masses of the people will exist in shameful barbarism if they are not given complete liberty to speak on any matter . . ." This is strong liberal theory. But Moreno finished the sentence thusly: ". . . as long as it is not in opposition to the holy truths of our august religion and the decisions of the government, which are always worthy of our greatest respect."[2]

These nineteenth century liberals were by our terms decidedly conservative in their political ideas. Usually their liberalism came first from their economics. They were liberal in the sense that they wanted the restrictions of mercantilism ended. Here they desired freedom, often what they referred to as freedom of trade. Moreno represented the Junta de Hacendados; on their behalf he wrote his memorable *Memorial of the Hacendados* in 1809, in which he argued for free trade with England. The large landowners needed free trade in order to sell their products, as did landowners in many other parts of Spanish America at the same time. It must have been an awkward moment for them, finding themselves on the liberal side of a central issue. On the other hand there were many merchants who traditionally came to liberalism earlier than the landowners and who now desired the perpetuation of monopoly and restricted trade. Clearly there are no easy ways to categorize. It is certain, however, that many of the leaders who did become liberals in the nineteenth century use of the term did so first because of economics. Their liberalism was usually more pronounced in economics than in the daily politics of government.

In fact, the issue of monarchy during the early nineteenth century is really quite academic. There were monarchists and republicans among the early leaders, just as in the United States, but the statesman who was irrevocably committed to one or the other form of government was rare indeed. Carrera of Chile was one of the few who were early committed to republicanism and who would have found it difficult to live in a monarchy. San Martín favored monarchy, although it does not appear that he became thoroughly convinced that monarchy was the best form of government for Peru until fairly late. By that time Bolívar had switched from his earlier monarchistic leanings to republicanism.

This difference between the two men was doubtless one of the reasons San Martín bowed out of the picture after the Guayaquil meeting.

These were the extremes. Most of the early statesmen seem to have preferred either the British system of limited monarchy or the United States variety of republicanism, but they were flexible and would have gotten along comfortably under either form of government. Much the same could be said about many of the founding fathers of the United States. The issue of monarchy was for many Spanish Americans a diplomatic tool rather than a life or death political decision. Men like Bernardo O'Higgins waved republicanism and monarchism around in an effort to attract recognition from either the United States or Great Britain. He gladly would have taken Chile either way if it would have meant recognition from one or the other of the great powers. And this seems to have been true of the majority of the early statesmen. They may have had their particular preferences, but as true classical liberals they would have been quite comfortable in either a republic or a limited monarchy. The issue to most of them was recognition by one of the major foreign powers. British recognition as early as 1818 or 1820 might have guaranteed a series of limited monarchies in Spanish America—any number that Britain would have deemed appropriate.

Their Political Theories

An examination of the political theories articulated during the independence period will illuminate the liberalism that informed the political structures of the emergent nations. For purposes of clarity and convenience these theories have been divided into four general categories: doctrinaire liberalism (in the nineteenth century sense), natural liberalism, doctrinaire federalism, and natural federalism. Doctrinaire liberalism was proposed especially by Francisco Miranda and Simón Bolívar. It was taken from the whole history of mankind and had little relevance to Spanish America. Miranda's constitutional schemes were never tried, and everywhere that Bolívar's exotic schemes were attempted they failed. Natural liberalism was the liberalism advocated outside the Bolivarian countries, and even within them when Bolívar was overruled. It was derived mostly from traditional political theory; but it was stimulated, and usually shaped, by the Enlightenment. Its most direct inspiration was the liberal 1812 Cádiz constitution, although the founding fathers were quite impressed with the United States example. Natural liberalism most effectively reflected the political needs of the active citizenry, and the constitutions it produced were the most enduring. Doctrinaire federalism was drawn from outside example, primarily by choice rather than need. The only time it was tried–in Venezuela in 1812–it failed. Natural federalism, the last of the four categories, is the most misunderstood of all Spanish American political expression. Its source was usually not the United States constitution, although the example was much appreciated and the document well known. Rather its source was traditional Spanish political theory and practice. It more accurately reflected the economic and political needs and desires of countries taken as a whole than did the other political theories. It was truly grass roots constitutionalism. Everywhere it was tried it failed, not because it was irrelevant or exotic–for it was overwhelmingly relevant and natural to the setting–but because in the final analysis the active citizenry in the various new nations found centralism the most efficacious means of governing. And centralism could be expressed quite naturally and effectively within the context of natural liberalism.

Doctrinaire Liberalism

The most ostentatious proponent of the irrelevant liberalism we have called doctrinaire was Francisco Miranda. Two decades before the independence movement actually commenced in Venezuela, Miranda had suggested to British officials the establishment of one independent government for all of Spanish America, including the territory from the Mississippi River to San Francisco Bay. At the head of the government would be a hereditary official, an Inca, called emperor. There would be a bicameral legislature. The upper house would be the senate, composed of lifetime appointees of the emperor (*caciques*). The lower house would be the chamber of communes, composed of men appointed by the emperor for five-year terms. They could be reappointed. The judiciary also would be appointed by the emperor, for lifetime terms.

By 1808 Miranda had toned down his plan somewhat, now proposing to British officials that four states be established on the "Colombian Continent." One would comprise Mexico and Guatemala; a second New Granada, Venezuela, and Quito; a third Peru and Chile; and a fourth la Plata. This later plan was proposed to Castlereagh early in 1808. By the middle of the year the British had thousands of troops prepared for a trip to northern South America to foment rebellion. But by July England and Spain had signed a formal peace, and these same troops were sent to Spain to aid the patriots against Napoleon's forces. One wonders what would have happened to Miranda's fanciful plans had the British sailed for South America, successfully started and guided a rebellion for independence, and then supervised the subsequent organic codes. They might well have become reality.

The most famous proponent of doctrinaire liberalism was Simón Bolívar, the towering figure of the Spanish American independence movement. Bolívar was a classical liberal and a great admirer of the British constitutional system. He took his constitutional ideas from the whole range of history; and although he firmly believed with Montesquieu that laws should reflect the particular characteristics of the country in which they are formulated, he often grafted artificial limbs on otherwise natural bodies. His views evolved and shifted as the independence movement progressed.

One of Bolívar's first major public statements on political theory and constitutions was his well-known Jamaica letter of 1815. In it he indicated a preference for paternal republics for Spanish America. He was not opposed to monarchy, but he considered the idea of a single monarch for all South America rather chimerical. He thought in 1815 that Mexico might perhaps become a constitutional monarchy, which in fact it did for a while. "If any American republic is to have a long life," he wrote, "I am inclined to believe it will be Chile." Again he was correct insofar as Chile was concerned, but other republics endured also. "Peru, on the contrary, contains two factors that clash with every just and liberal principle: gold and slaves. The former corrupts everything; the latter are themselves corrupt. The soul of a serf can seldom really appreciate true freedom. Either he loses his head in uprisings of his self-respect in chains. . . . I imagine that in Lima the rich will not tolerate democracy, nor will the freed slaves and *pardos* [mulattoes] accept aristocracy. The former will prefer the tyranny of a single man, to avoid the tumult of rebellion and to provide, at least, a peaceful system. If Peru intends to recover her independence, she has much to do."[3] He was not far wrong about Peru either.

His own ideas on government in 1815 were expressed when it came to New Granada. He thought that New Granada would unite with Venezuela if they both agreed to form a central republic. "Its government might follow the English pattern, except that in place of a king there will be an executive who will be elected, at most, for life, but his office will never be hereditary, if a republic is desired."[4] There would be a hereditary upper chamber or senate and a lower chamber modeled after the House of Commons.

In 1815 Bolívar strongly desired a "union" of Spanish American states as the best means of guaranteeing independence. This would become one of his favorite themes. Finally, at his insistence, a congress of American states met in Panama in 1826, but it was neither well attended nor well supported. With the advantage of hindsight we know that a confederation of Spanish American states was merely a dream.

By early 1819 Bolívar had established leadership over the various rebel bands, including the *llaneros* under Páez, and had set up headquarters at Angostura, on the Orinoco River. He even called for a congress to meet at Angostura to draft a constitution for Venezuela, which had not yet been reconquered. In February he addressed the congress and gave further indication of his political views. Now he was a thoroughgoing republican, even arguing that frequent elections are necessary to prevent one man from gaining too much power. But at the same time he argued that the executive in a republic required greater authority than a constitutional monarch. In fact, "let the entire system of government be strengthened. . . . Precisely because no form of government is so weak as the democratic, its framework must be firmer . . ." Again he desired a legislature that would follow the British example, including a hereditary senate. The judiciary would be rather traditional. And now there would be a fourth branch—a moral power. Bolívar not only lectured the delegates on the constitutional history of the world, he proposed the establishment of an Areopagus, taken from the experience of Athens, Rome, and Sparta! It was to be a body of censors, "having jurisdiction over the youth, the hearts of men, public spirit, good customs, and republican ethics."[5]

The delegates at the congress of Angostura were manifestly less doctrinaire than Bolívar and not as much under his influence as one might imagine, considering the setting. They adopted his plan for a constitution, but with serious modifications; for instance, they dropped the fourth branch. Bolívar had urged a hereditary senate, but the delegates granted senators only life terms. The president's term of office perhaps followed Bolívar's plan. Presidents would serve a four-year term and could be reelected for one term before having to step down for at least a term. The final constitution, without the Liberator's exotic trimmings, was very much like other liberal codes of the period, and as such it placed strong emphasis on the protection of private property. This constitution, like many other liberal codes of the period, openly recognized two classes of citizens: active and passive. One of the qualifications for active citizenship, which meant the privilege of voting, was the ability to read and write; but this qualification would not go into effect until 1830. That is, the delegates, with their liberal belief in the efficacy of legislation, were giving the uneducated a decade in which to get educated and thus participate in the suffrage. This was certainly reasonable to the nineteenth century liberal.

Bolívar was selected to be the first president, and Francisco Antonio Zea, of New Granada was to be his vice-president. Shortly after these proceedings Bolívar took his troops into New Granada and defeated the Spaniards at Boyacá. With this great success Bolívar induced the congress at Angostura–which already included delegates from parts of New Granada–to proclaim the creation of a new state, comprising the former viceroyalty of New Granada and the former captaincy general of Venezuela. It was called the republic of Colombia, with Cúcuta its provisional capital. The republic was divided into three departments, each with a vice-president chosen by the congress. Bolívar was selected as president.

In 1821 a congress at Cúcuta wrote a constitution for the republic of Gran Colombia. It is difficult to gauge Bolívar's influence over the delegates. The president was given a four-year term, with one immediate reelection possible, and senators were given eight-year terms. One would think that Bolívar would have desired longer terms for the senators. The constitution was not burdened by any of the Liberator's earlier alien trappings. Francisco de Paula Santander became vice-president, and Bolívar became president, although he soon left his active post to continue the independence movement.

From Colombia Bolívar carried the independence movement into Peru, but he did not become that country's president until 1826. Prior to this he wrote his most celebrated constitution, the one for Bolivia. Upper Peru had been under the control of one of the Liberator's lieutenants, José Antonio Sucre. In 1825 an assembly called by Sucre declared the independence of this region that soon came to be known as Bolivia. Bolívar wrote the new country's constitution, and this document represents the second stage of the Liberator's political development. Whereas to about 1825 he had inclined toward senatorial rule, now he favored the presidency, which he thought should be a life term. The Bolivian constitution provided for a legislature of three houses: tribunes, senators, and censors. Again Bolívar wanted his Areopagus, and this time he got it. The censors were to preside over education and the press. They were given life terms. Tribunes were to serve for four years and senators for eight. The president was given a life term, and he could choose his successor. The country was divided into departments, each administered by a prefect; the departments were divided into provinces, administered by governors; and the provinces were divided into cantons, administered by corregidors. Notwithstanding the exotic frills, the constitution was much like the other liberal documents of the period, with strong emphasis on individual freedoms and property rights.

With only minor changes the constitution was adopted. As soon as he finished the documents Bolívar returned to Peru. Sucre was given executive authority, having agreed to serve for two years. He was an honest and earnest administrator, but the problems confronting the new country were too great for him. One of the most serious was that it was difficult to pay the troops, always a touchy situation but especially so in an infant state. In one military uprising Sucre was even wounded. In 1828 he gave up his position and left the country he helped found. Shortly thereafter he was murdered. Administrative changes in Bolivia for the next century and a half would be quite irregular, to say the least.

Bolívar wanted Peru to adopt the Bolivian constitution. The Peruvians agreed to do so, but only under the condition that he accept the presidency. The constitution was adopted with minor changes, and Bolívar became president of Peru. But almost immediately he left Peru for Colombia, where things were not going well. The chamber of censors lasted only a few months in Peru until it was thrown out. Early in 1827 the government itself was overthrown by the military. The following year a new constitution was proclaimed; it called for a two-chamber legislature and a president who would be permitted a four-year term with one immediate reelection.

By the time Bolívar reached Bogotá, the republic of Gran Colombia was already straining at the seams and was nearly ready to break up. In Bogotá he actively assumed the presidency and tried to put things in order. Soon he went to Caracas, where he managed to keep a fractious Páez in line. In 1827 he was back in Bogotá, and now he wanted a new constitution. Consequently a constitutional assembly met at Ocaña in 1828; but the majority of delegates were not under the Liberator's influence, and they refused to change the old constitution. Bolívar withdrew his own delegates and soon broke with Santander. Ocaña was the beginning of the end for the Liberator. Shortly, an assassination attempt was made on Bolívar's life, with one of the results being that Santander was sent into exile. Because Peru had invaded Ecuador, Bolívar felt it necessary to leave Bogotá and travel to that troubled area. By the time he returned his position in Bogotá had grown tenuous. In late 1829 Páez took Venezuela out of the republic of Gran Colombia, and soon Juan José Flores did the same with Ecuador. In March 1830 Bolívar resigned, and soon thereafter he died. Santander arrived back in Bogotá in 1832 and was elected president of New Granada, a post he held for four years.

Miranda and Bolívar were not the only advocates of what we have called doctrinaire liberalism (a liberalism taken from books and the study of history, a political theory that was not suited to the environment for which it was intended and that was everywhere short-lived); they were just the most famous and, in Bolívar's case, the most influential. Other Spanish Americans also were doctrinaire in their approach, and so too were some foreign travelers and diplomats. Especially notorious in this category was the United States agent in Chile, Joel Roberts Poinsett. A compulsive advocate of his country's form of government, he went out of his way to contact leading Chileans and convince them of the need for a constitution, particularly one modeled on the United States example. He even drafted a constitution and presented it to José Miguel Carrera, the man who controlled the Santiago government, in July 1812. True to its precepts it called for an administration of three branches, with the executive being a *gran jefe* (great chief). Not surprisingly, the Chilean counterpart of the United States president would be at least thirty-six years old. It is remarkable that Poinsett should display such little political acumen: Carrera was only twenty-eight at the time! The document was not accepted.

Natural Liberalism

Natural liberalism was adopted readily by the Spanish American independence leaders; it perfectly suited their nature, fulfilled their needs, and buttressed their aspirations. It often resembled the liberalism of the founding fathers of the United States and their constitution, but only in the sense that the United States was an inspiring example and its constitution served often as a structural (as opposed to substantive) model. The central source of early nineteenth century Spanish American liberalism was traditional Spanish political theory as updated by the Enlightenment and as presented finally in several organic codes of the era, most notably the 1812 constitution of Cádiz.

The Cádiz constitution culminated the liberal movement in Enlightenment Spain. It provided for limited constitutional monarchy. Its essence was notably Spanish, but its ideas were couched in the vocabulary of the French revolutionary constitutions. When the *Cortes* met in 1812 there were very few written constitutions in the world. Four of them were French: those of 1791, 1793, 1795, and 1799. The French codes were doubtless influenced in turn by the United States constitution, but the Cádiz delegates quite often took their wording directly from one or another of the French documents. Many clauses were direct translations from the French constitutions. But this does not mean that the Cádiz delegates were lifting ideas; rather they were simply and expeditiously seeking the vehicles through which they might express their own views, their concepts of traditional Spanish political theory as developed by the Spanish bourgeoisie and seasoned by the European Enlightenment, or, to put it another way, the concepts of the Enlightenment as seasoned by traditional Spanish bourgeois political theory.

While the Cádiz delegates were liberal they were not at all democratic. They might end press censorship and restrict the activities of the church, but they were indeed conservative by modern standards; and, in fact, they adopted a limited monarchy. The liberal decrees of the constitutional convention fired up many marginal patriots in the colonies and converted them to active participants in the independence movement. But the decrees of the 1812 period, contrary to those of the 1820 period, were not liberal enough to convert the upper clergy to independence. One step taken by the *Cortes* was a great boon to the independence movement. It had been estimated at the time of the *Cortes* that fifteen to sixteen million people lived in the Spanish American colonies and the Philippines and that only about ten and a half million lived in Spain itself. Thus representation in the *Cortes*, and in future parliamentary bodies, based on an individual head count would have given a majority of votes to the colonists and not the resident Spaniards. Article 22 of the constitution permitted the exclusion of the colored castes from the status of citizenship and therefore from the head count. The article was passed after a vigorous debate by a vote of 108 to 36, at a time when there were more than 50 Spanish American delegates at the *Cortes*. Some colonists did not vote on the measure, and it seems that some voted for it. Nonetheless, racial discrimination against blacks had been incorporated into the constitution. This turned out to be a great propaganda tool for the independence leaders in the colonies; it served well in encouraging Spanish Americans with African blood to join the movement.

As the Cádiz constitution relied heavily for its wording on the French revolutionary constitutions, so the Spanish American constitutions often relied heavily on the Cádiz document. Because the Spanish Americans almost always chose republicanism does not mean they copied the United States constitution. For their thoughts on life, liberty, and property they did not have to refer to any constitution; but for an easy and lucid way of expressing these thoughts they naturally turned to the Spanish and French constitutions and to the Declaration of the Rights of Man.

The liberalism of the Spanish American founding fathers was expressed in both centralist and federalist constitutions. Both were logical and culminating expressions of the active citizenry that produced them. The federalist constitutions were the more interesting in the sense that they were usually more innovative, better attuned to the needs of the countries as a whole, and more nearly a reflection of the aspirations of marginal power groups. They were natural outgrowths of the Spanish American colonial experience; but they were not able to satisfy the desires of controlling power blocs in the new countries, and everywhere they failed. Very often centralism spelled dominance of a capital region and relegation of provinces to a secondary status. This was unfortunate because centralism could also contribute toward political stability and economic growth.

A discussion of some of the early constitutions will permit an appreciation of the character of the political thinking—the liberalism—that informed the period. For the moment we shall concentrate on constitutions that were either mainly or generally centralist.

Chile and Uruguay were the only two countries to write constitutions by 1833 that lasted until the twentieth century. Both were centralist. The Argentine constitution of 1853 was the longest-lived of all Spanish American organic codes, and although it had certain federalist trappings it was quite effectively a centralist document.

Chile had its first constitution, a provisional document, as early as 1812. It was a short code that gave executive authority to a three-man junta. But the executive authority was sharply limited by a senate of seven members. Thus we already see one of the central characteristics of Chilean constitutional history: Strong executives were balanced by strong congresses.

Chile's next constitution was promulgated in 1818, after the country had won and declared its independence. It also was a provisional document. Until a congress was called (and as it turned out that was not for several years) the legislative branch comprised only a senate of five members, selected by the supreme director, Bernardo O'Higgins. The senators received substantial annual stipends of two thousand pesos but were forbidden to hold other public employment. Any citizen more than thirty years old, "of exalted patriotism, of integrity, prudence . . ." was eligible for membership. The only serious qualification was age. Since members of the active citizenry were going to elect government officials from among their own number, no more specific qualifications were necessary. Democracy was not an issue at the moment, and as a political ideology it had few, if any, articulate supporters. The primary purpose of the senate was to insure observance of the constitution. It was given the broad and effective powers that a legislature should possess in a republican form of government. Senate approval was required on all important matters, such as "imposing taxes, soliciting loans, declaring war, making peace, forming treaties of alliance, commerce, neutrality; sending ambassadors, consuls, deputies or envoys to foreign powers; raising new troops or sending them outside the State;

undertaking public works and creating new authorities or employs." The senate could pass a law over the supreme director's veto. Provision was made for amending the constitution.

This constitution is a much misinterpreted document. Since the senators were not elected—they were appointed by the supreme director—it has appeared that the supreme director in reality created a specious legislature to lend respectability to his regime. It is often suggested that O'Higgins reserved unlimited powers for himself. At best this may have been his intent. There is little evidence to indict or absolve him on this point. However, as it turned out, the senate proved to be a viable, energetic legislature.

The constitution provided that the present supreme director would continue his tenure but that later directors would be elected by the provinces for a term to be determined by a future law. Qualifications for the position were similar to those of the senate. The supreme director's privileges were the standard and familiar ones of nineteenth century presidents. The customary contemporary civil liberties were guaranteed. A previous congressional decree declaring children born to slaves to be free was repeated, but there was no special section on citizenship. Nothing was included to eliminate the Indian from citizenship, and in a negative manner the document thus granted that citizenship. Everyone was instructed to follow the moral principle "*No hagas a otro lo que no quieres hagan contigo*"—the golden rule that was repeated in many constitutions of the period.

The heart of the Chilean liberal system was the senate, as later it would be the congress. This was also true of the rest of republican Spanish America. Far too much has been made of the powers of the presidents—perhaps because at times they undermined the liberal structures and drew extreme powers to themselves—to the point that there has often been a failure to perceive the importance of congresses in the vision of the founding fathers. Strong congresses, as in the Chilean case, contributed mightily to political stability. The strength and independence of the Chilean senate created by the constitution of 1818 tells us a good deal about Chilean liberalism. This body constantly reviewed the supreme director's actions and often overruled him on critical issues.

There are few studies of the actual relations between senates and congresses on the one side and executive authorities on the other. Present information indicates that the Chilean example was not particularly exceptional, especially when compared with the experience of other countries in which there was a rather broad and well-integrated capitalist class, such as Mexico, Uruguay, Argentina, and Venezuela. During the early decades of the nineteenth century the active citizenry were impressed with and fought for balanced government. Once governments failed and political instability ensued they were at times willing to suffer extreme executive authority, as did the later positivists in Mexico, in order to gain the general stability necessary for them to carry out their economic activities. But for the moment the active citizenry in Spanish America had an essential predilection for balanced government.

Chile's next constitution was drafted in 1822. It was the last year of O'Higgins's tenure. The document provided all the familiar personal guarantees. All Chileans were equal before the law, and, in consequence, all were required to contribute toward the costs of government according to their means. On the surface, citizenship was rather inclusive. Citizens were those born in Chile and married, or single and at least twenty-five years old, or those who were married to a Chilean and could prove three years of residence in the country. But to be a citizen one had to be able to read and write, an expected manifestation of the liberal ideology that runs through the document. The reading and writing requirement was designed not to apply until 1833. That is, a ten-year period of grace was extended to those who as yet could not read and write. But also quite typical of the liberal thought of the day was the easy manner in which one might lose his citizenship. For instance, anyone employed as a domestic servant, or who did not have a known way of supporting himself, or who was in debt to the public treasury would be deprived of his citizenship so long as any of these conditions prevailed. The religion of the nation was declared to be Roman Catholic, to the exclusion of any other.

The government was republican and representative. The three familiar branches were established, with the legislature now being bicameral—comprising a chamber of deputies and a court of representatives. To be elected deputy one had to be a citizen and possess property with a value of not less than two thousand pesos. The chamber was granted broad powers and was clearly the more powerful of the two legislative houses, very much resembling the unicameral legislative body created by the 1812 Cádiz constitution.

The court of representatives was a permanent body of seven members elected by the chamber. At least four had to be deputies. While the chamber was in session the court became a senate and was devised to complement the legislative activities of the chamber, but when it was not in session the court of representatives was charged with guarding the constitution. At such times it could approve or create provisional legislation, and in extraordinary times it could convoke the chamber into session. As liberals, the framers of the constitution were particularly concerned with protecting constitutional freedoms; and the court, though it may have smacked of reaction to a democrat, was an appropriate instrument to guarantee these freedoms while the chamber was not in session. The legislative branch had already established a proprietary primacy in government during the O'Higgins years and now was merely writing this reality into law.

The degree to which the Chileans were not influenced by the United States example is perhaps best illustrated in the nature of the cabinet. It was composed of ministers, not all of whom were appointed by the supreme director. For instance, all bishops were ministers, and each university was required to select one doctor to serve as a minister. Two merchants and two *hacendados* (large landowners), with a capital of not less than thirty thousand pesos, were to be appointed ministers by the chamber of deputies. The supreme director was required to select the remaining ministers from specific categories, such as the army.

Assessed merely on the surface, the constitution surely gives the impression that a governing oligarchy was attempting to insure its own longevity. The term *oligarchy* should be used with extreme caution in referring to this period of Spanish American history. The oligarchy was not monolithic, and the government created by the new organic law was intended to be fairly representative of it.

Rather than a president, the constitution provided for a supreme director, whose faculties and limitations were quite similar to both his counterpart in the United States and the constitutional monarch created by the Cádiz constitution. It was an elective position with a special note making it perfectly certain that it, unlike the Spanish monarchy, was not hereditary. The term of office was six years, but the supreme director could be reelected for another four-year term. In the future the legislature would elect the supreme director with a two-thirds majority, but for the present it was stipulated that O'Higgins would serve as supreme director for a full term beginning with the swearing of allegiance to the document.

The constitution officially divided Chile into the now standard three provinces, each to be administered by a governor-intendant. But the framers of the document desired to centralize administrative control more than in the past. Thus the entire country was divided into departments, each to be governed by an official named by the supreme director "with the title directorial delegate." More than any other aspect of the constitution this article led to the overthrow of the O'Higgins regime. The provinces of Concepción and Coquimbo were affronted by this insidious attempt to subvert prerogatives which since 1810 had begun to seem traditional. The spirit of regionalism inherent in the Spanish colonial system had been energized during the decade after 1810 when provincial juntas controlled their regions much as they chose.

These highlights of the constitution of 1822 should demonstrate just how patently liberal were the representatives of the active citizenry. Their central concern was constitutional government, the creation of an organic law that would guarantee individual freedoms. They were humanitarians in the sense that a pervasive sentiment of *noblesse oblige* compelled them to take an interest in the welfare of all members of society, but they were not democrats and were not inspired by supernal concepts of social reform.

A provincial rebellion threw O'Higgins out of office in January 1823. The same year Chile had a new constitution. There was a federalist interlude in 1826 and another central code in 1828. The next constitution that should be considered is the one of 1833, which lasted until 1925.

In no other country in Spanish America was the bourgeoisie so well integrated and balanced as in Chile. In no other country had the commercial class—the merchants—become so politically powerful. They were politically important not only in the capital and in a chief port or two but throughout the country. While all constitutions of the period were highly reflective of bourgeois sentiments and needs, no other one quite so neatly reflected the ascendancy of the commercial class in society.

Credit for the success of the constitution of 1833 is generally given to Diego Portales, the merchant son of the former superintendent of the royal mint in Santiago, who organized the *pelucón* government (as it was called) after the battle of Lircay in 1829. Portales is supposed to have dominated the *pelucón* government and created an authoritarian presidential state based on an alliance of the landed oligarchy, the military, and the clergy. In reality, the core of the *pelucón* alliance was the merchants and that large intermixed group of merchants, miners, and landowners. While we may make only a tentative statement at the moment, it is probably true that Chile was the first Spanish American country to have a fully successful bourgeois revolution; and it is in the role of the bourgeoisie that we will probably find the clue to Chile's relative progress and stability during the nineteenth century.

Portales himself was never president and had somewhat less influence in the *pelucón* government than is generally supposed; and he had precious little to do with the drafting and adopting of the constitution. In fact, the government itself did not either draft a proposal for the constitution or support in any unified manner one of the three drafts presented by different delegates at the constitutional convention. But Portales did set the pattern and tone of the new government shortly after the pelucones seized power. The new government was to be pointedly civilian and impersonal. One of Portales's first steps was to reduce the size of the military officialdom and to create a civil militia as a counterpoise. Other merchants, such as Manuel Rengifo, became the heart of the new bureaucracy; and the evidence indicates that they owed their personal allegiance not to the president, but to the system.

Although presidents, serving generally two consecutive five-year terms, did indeed have renowned power and did control patronage, the regimes in office down to the end of the century appear to have been more rational-legal than paternalistic. The reason for the Chilean success was not that the paternalistic king had been reinstated in the form of a paternalistic president but that precisely the opposite had occurred: A mixed colonial system was replaced by an impressively impersonal, rational system. And this was accomplished in part by giving the Chilean congress strikingly vital power. Wherever anything like a bourgeois revolution had taken place—in countries like Argentina, Chile, Mexico, Colombia, Venezuela, and Uruguay—faith was placed not only in strong executives but also in strong congresses.

The Chilean constitutions were notably typical of the other liberal organic codes of the period. There were naturally local variations, but in central respects they were all generally quite alike. The Chilean constitution of 1828 abolished entailed estates and the constitution of 1833 reinstated them; the one of 1828 made provision for provinces and the succeeding code abolished provinces. Yet running through both documents, as well as others of the period–like the Mexican constitution of Apatzingán of 1814 and the Uruguayan constitution of 1830–was a vigorous emphasis on law and order, the protection of individual freedoms, and the sanctity of private property. Even when a constitution might aim to restrict large landed estates it would still emphatically protect private property rights in general. In one way or another they all mentioned and were dedicated to the theme stated in the Argentine code of 1815: "*la Libertad, la Igualdad, la Propiedad y la Seguridad*."

Doctrinaire Federalism

The only constitution of the period that created a federal state artificially and academically was the Venezuelan code of 1811, which lasted only about a year, although it was not superseded for a while. By the time Venezuela declared its independence (that is, Caracas declared independence for itself and part of the captaincy general) Francisco Miranda was a major force in local politics. In 1808 he had presented a plan to the *cabildo* of Caracas that called for a federal government. He planned a unicameral legislature and a dual executive. There is no doubt that the federal constitution adopted in December of 1811 was inspired to a considerable degree by Miranda. But it is clear also that the delegates were influenced by the United States constitution and the constitutions of several of the North American states. The delegates had in their hands Thomas Paine's *La Independencia de la Costa Firme* . . . , translated by Manuel García de Seña and published in Philadelphia in 1811. Appended were translations of the United States constitution and those of Massachusetts, Pennsylvania, and Virginia. In addition to these sources the delegates also borrowed from the French revolutionary documents. It should be borne in mind that this Venezuelan code was written before the Cádiz constitution of 1812.

The reason this federal constitution was doctrinaire is that it was the creation of the capital district and not the provinces, as would have been natural in this case. It was quite unnatural for capitals of colonies in general to desire federalism; their best interests, they thought, resided in centralist states, which they could better control. However, in the large and unwieldy political entity of New Granada some residents of Bogotá, the capital of the old viceroyalty, were federalists because they thought political power would shift away from Bogotá in a centralist state.

But this is not to say that the constitution was not a typically liberal document, for this it was. It also was dedicated to the preservation and enhancement of the fundamental rights of man: "*la libertad, la igualdad, la propiedad y la seguridad.*" Like so many other codes of the period this one attempted to establish civil authority over the military, and it did so in part by emphasizing the importance of a civil militia: "A well regulated and trained militia, composed of the citizenry, is the most suitable and secure natural defense of a free State." But perhaps because of Miranda's influence the constitution provided for a three-man executive authority. Since the first republic endured only a year, a half year after the completion of the constitution of 1811, one wonders what would have been its fate under normal conditions. On more than one occasion Bolívar later stated that the failure of the constitution was the plural executive. When he returned to Caracas in 1813 he established an equally impermanent centralist regime.

Natural Federalism

Natural federalism was the brand of federalism advocated by the provinces; it was their way of establishing a liberal republic that was balanced not only within the administration but also among the provinces —which is to say that the provinces aimed to somewhat neutralize the generally commanding power and influence of the capital regions. This kind of federalism responded to the needs of whole countries rather than only the capitals. It was the most interesting and creative constitutionalism of the independence era. But it failed everywhere because capital regions (though they also often had some federalists), with their vested interests and traditional authority, were too powerful for the provincial leaders, who were not always united in their efforts and who anyway often depended on the capitals for revenue derived from foreign trade. It failed also because capital regions seemed to have the will and resources to provide calm and stability, whereas federation often led to local autonomy, a usually awkward situation for capitalists.

The matter of federalism was not always a question of liberalism versus conservatism. Among early nineteenth century liberals there were people who obviously were more liberal or more conservative than others. The more liberal ones often advocated federalism. The centralist forces were generally more interested in stability and the easy flow of business than they were in an equitable sharing of power and resources. In the general scheme of things they may have been relatively more conservative than others before they thought about centralism or federalism; once they made the choice for centralism they were usually identified with the more conservative elements. On the other hand, the federalists often turned out to be liberals, not always because it suited their personalities but because their attitudes on central states often brought them to more radical positions than they might otherwise have reached.

Yet occasionally federalism meant conservative reaction. Turning power over to the provinces meant to some the opportunity of local one-man or family rule. At times liberals understood this and advocated centralism. All three constitutional projects considered by the convention that drafted Chile's code of 1833 provided for provincial assemblies, and they were approved by the delegates. However, a while later Manuel José Gandarillas, editor of the government's official paper, *El Araucano*, but an active public critic of the conservative point of view at the convention, proposed the abolition of provincial assemblies. The convention discussed the motion on one day and adopted it on the next. All previous articles dealing with provincial assemblies were thus thrown out. Among government leaders Gandarillas was considered something of an ultra liberal. More than any other of the active participants of the convention, Gandarillas held the line for preservation of the truly liberal features of the constitution of 1828, and he gave the new constitution one of its most enduring characteristics—that of the creator of a strong central government. Gandarillas was one of those liberals who understood that provincial assemblies could be anything but liberal at times.

The problems surrounding the federalist-centralist debate and controversy were among the gravest faced by many of the new nations. Some of them, like Chile, managed to solve them quite expeditiously and effectively; but others, like Argentina, had a more difficult and unsettling time of it. Even where the question of federalism or centralism did not frustrate stability for long, as in Chile, a working formula had to be arrived at. It is no wonder that so many of the early Chilean leaders, supreme directors, presidents, and revolts came from the south. Other countries had a more difficult time working out a solution. The relationship between the federalist-centralist controversy and stability will be taken up in the following chapter. For the moment we are still interested in the political ideas represented by federalism. Two examples will further an understanding of these ideas.

Uruguay The Banda Oriental fell under the jurisdiction of the viceroyalty of the Río de la Plata, whose capital was Buenos Aires. Yet Montevideo was the more natural port and was the first port of call for ships arriving from Europe and sailing up the Plate River. There was thus a great rivalry between the merchants of Montevideo and Buenos Aires. The crown itself recognized the value of Montevideo and rewarded it with special privileges. But the majority of merchants dealing in European trade resided in the capital, and in 1794 a *consulado* was established there. It controlled trade for the entire viceroyalty, and it gave the Buenos Aires merchants an excessive advantage over their Montevideo competitors. One of the results of this commercial rivalry, with the cards stacked in favor of the viceregal capital, was that when Buenos Aires struck out for independence Montevideo became the mainstay of loyalist sentiment in the Plate area. And when Montevideo did decide upon independence it wanted a federalist confederation and not a centralist state to be created out of the old viceroyalty.

The leader of the federalist movement in the Banda Oriental was José Gervasio Artigas. It was he who brought Montevideo and the provinces of the Banda Oriental together in the effort to become independent from both Spain and Buenos Aires. In 1813 a constituent assembly met at Buenos Aires for the purpose of drafting a constitution for the former viceroyalty. The Banda Oriental therefore had its own congress to decide on the position to be taken by its delegates to the Buenos Aires assembly. Artigas addressed the Oriental representatives and presented his own plan for a federalist confederation. It was perhaps the most extreme statement of federalism made during the entire Spanish American independence period. The Banda Oriental would maintain an extraordinary degree of autonomy in what Artigas conceived of as a confederation. He took pains to insure that Buenos Aires would not dominate trade in the Plate region.

The Oriental assembly drafted a set of instructions for its delegates to the Buenos Aires convention. Because the port of Montevideo was still held by the Spaniards they called for the opening of the ports of Maldonado and Colonia to international trade. The commander of the British naval forces in the region would be invited to protect British ships taking advantage of the new policy. True to Artigas's wishes the instructions provided for a confederation granting maximum autonomy to the individual provinces. They stated that Buenos Aires must not become the capital of the new confederation. The instructions not only provided for the relative independence of the Provincia Oriental within the proposed confederation, they called for the complete independence of the confederation from Spain, without any regard for the Spanish crown. It is interesting that of the five delegates the assembly elected to the Buenos Aires convention, four were priests.

Buenos Aires wanted centralism; the Oriental delegates were refused admittance to the Buenos Aires convention. Buenos Aires was doomed to failure for the moment. The Argentine littoral provinces, those of Entre Ríos, Corrientes, and Santa Fe, which were served by the great Argentine rivers, felt much the same about Buenos Aires as did Artigas They soon joined him in his Liga Federal and the fight against Buenos Aires hegemony.

The Orientals not only had to draft instructions for their representatives to the Buenos Aires convention, they had to decide upon a constitution for their own province. They too drafted their constitution in 1813, for the Provincia Oriental del Uruguay. It was a document very much like the other liberal codes of the period, again with strong emphasis on the protection of individual rights and freedoms.

Mexico Many provincial Mexicans desired a federalist state so that the overweening power of the capital might be lessened and regional economic development made possible. For instance, there was a glaring rivalry between the Veracruz and Mexico City merchants during the late colonial period. And to the north of Veracruz residents of the Tampico region wanted their port improved and opened to international trade. A Mexican delegate to the Cádiz convention published a book there in 1812 (which was republished in Mexico in 1813) that called for a federalist approach to Mexico's economic development. Specifically, he wanted benefits for the north-central region. The basis of Mexican federalism was fundamentally economic. Steps were taken by the crown to improve regional facilities, including the opening of the port of Tampico to international trade, but once independence was achieved the issue of federalism flared, with the result being the federalist constitution of 1824.

Independent Mexico's first constitution was indeed federalist. Major power was focused in the central government, but the states were given substantial authority. The constitution provided for a liberal republic that resembled the North American example. However, the inspiration for Mexican federalism was not so much the United States as it was Spanish and French political experience. In fact, Mexicans seem to have been more impressed with French federalist theorists than with the North American founding fathers.

The federal constitution of 1824 was noticeably typical of other liberal organic codes of the period, and with its emphasis on individual freedoms and property rights it was a lineal descendant of the Apatzingán constitution of 1814. The constitution endured only about a decade, when it was replaced by a centralist code. Yet during this decade and even thereafter under centralist regimes many advocates of federalism became powerful national figures and attempted to attend to the needs of the provinces. Often leaders with profoundly liberal leanings, like Valentín Gómez Farías and Benito Juárez, got their start in national politics from regional governorships.

Federalism too was liberalism, although at times it meant different things to different provincial leaders; but it was not efficacious enough to provide the stability inherent in a centralist regime or to satisfy the demands of the powerful residents of the capital districts.

Conclusion

One should not think of the new national societies as being dominated by a group of conservative landed aristocrats, who with their clerical and military support were essentially dilettantes at government, and who sought stability and order rather than progress. For one thing, the term *conservative* is misleading when applied to the early nineteenth century. For another, the landed aristocracy did not generally dominate and control the new national societies and governments exclusively even in the smaller countries that later became coffee or banana republics. In fact, many members of the landed aristocracy might well be included in the bourgeoisie that was, depending on the time and place, more or less integrated. While agrarians as a group were notoriously partial to stability, and many of them (often a majority) practiced a brand of economics that displayed feudal overtones, others were conspicuously profit oriented and involved in promoting scientific and technical progress and in supporting political regimes that were liberal-conservative—in twentieth century terms—rather than reactionary. And one should not forget that from the ranks of the landed oligarchy the United States drew some of its most famous and brilliant political theorists, men who were often clearly classical liberals in the Lockean tradition. So too did Spanish America.

Notes

1. Quoted in José Luis Romero, *A History of Argentine Political Thought* (Stanford, 1963), p. 70.

2. Ibid.

3. Quoted in David Bushnell (ed.), *The Liberator, Simón Bolivar* (New York, 1970), pp. 11-21.

4. Ibid., pp. 23-36.

5. Ibid.

CHAPTER SIX

The Problems of Independent Statehood

Many of the problems faced by the new nations of Spanish America are well known and have been celebrated by countless writers. For a long while now emphasis has been placed on the issues of geography, transportation, race, praetorianism, lack of qualified administrative personnel, lack of political experience, the disruptive church versus state question, and the problem of centralism versus federalism. These were all truly real and serious problems; indeed they throttled progress and often threatened stability. Lately many writers have seized upon the issue of colonialism and neocolonialism as the central cause of retardation and even instability in the new countries. These writers place more emphasis on the difficulties of a neocolonial nation in a world capitalist system than they do on the other more traditionally mentioned problems. For convenience we may divide the problems confronting the new nations into two broad categories: those relating to the special issue of neocolonialism and world capitalism and those of a general administrative nature. It is the intent of this chapter to examine some of the problems in both categories in the hope of providing a better understanding of the texture of early national life in Spanish America and of the difficulties of independent statehood. It is hoped also that this understanding will suggest a new perspective on recent problems.

First, though, a word about the general concept of stability. North Americans have always been quite impressed by political stability, and we have been inclined to view stability and progress in other countries from the perspective of the United States. Yet extralegal changes in government have not always been any more disruptive to the daily life of a country's citizenry than our civil and world wars and police actions. Some Spanish American countries during the nineteenth century witnessed long periods of political, economic, and social stability through the establishment of dictatorships. At times these dictatorships produced a stability around which societies and economies stagnated; at other times the stability they wrought generated growth and a certain degree of dynamism. It is unwise to label whole periods instable or chaotic unless we take the trouble to explain exactly what these terms mean, and how such instability or chaos affected the normal functioning of the society. There is very little research to guide us here. It is certain, however, that we have been much too impressed with coups and revolts and too little impressed with the degree societies were unaffected by them.

The New States and World Capitalism

It is only recently that the problems of the emergent nations have been placed in the perspective of world capitalism. The Spanish American countries had been colonies for centuries, and with relatively little warning they were thrust upon the world capitalist scene. There was little alternative for them at the moment. They might have joined in some form of common market, formed a sort of economic league; but in 1810 or 1820 they could not have become socialist or joined a world socialist system, because there was none of this then. They had to become capitalist states; and they had to compete in the world capitalist system. For this awesome task they were not always well prepared, but they were better prepared than one might think. Their merchant, mining, and agrarian economies fit quite well into the world capitalist system; actually they had been part of it all along. While the new countries were no longer colonies they were peripheries or satellites to the world capitalist metropolises.

This reality has led to a labeling of the new situation as one of neocolonialism, and in at least three critical ways it was neocolonialism. First, a good deal of the capital produced by local regions within individual countries was expropriated by the metropolis of the new state. In turn much of the capital absorbed by the national metropolis was expropriated by the world capitalist metropolises, located especially in Great Britain and the United States. Second, economies geared to the world capitalist market did not develop in a balanced, integrated manner; they were therefore increasingly at the mercy of the idiosyncrasies of that market. This meant that the new nations did not develop industrial self-sufficiency or at least a creditable industrial sector—a point that has been particularly disturbing to recent nationalists. And finally, when a new nation depends heavily on revenues from exports, and imports nearly all of its commodities, both prices and economic priorities will often be determined outside the nation itself. Foreign values therefore will tend to modulate and characterize the nature of the developing national societies, and one of a truly independent and distinct nature might not develop to maturity.

But this is not the whole picture. The fact is that though one must lament the inequities of a world capitalist system, national societies did emerge with their own identities and with their own nationalism that at times carried them into international wars. And although balanced economies are desirable, recent experience suggests that had the new nations been singularly socialist or part of a world socialist system their plight might have been the same. There can be neocolonialism in a socialist system just as easily as in a capitalist system, especially on a worldwide basis. And one should bear in mind that protectionism and socialism are not synonymous terms; socialists also may be free traders. So far as the expropriation of capital goes, one is left with the facts that the metropolis-satellite schema suggests economic development and not stagnation and that capital did accumulate within national economies, immensely more than is usually supposed.

A further examination of the question of neocolonialism will permit it to be placed in a proper perspective and will allow a more accurate understanding of the problems of independent statehood.

Neither the economies nor the societies of the new nations were entirely well suited to the requirements of a world capitalist system. The active citizenry thrived on capitalism, and although they were often surrounded by foreigners—merchants, miners, and even at times industrialists—they acquitted themselves remarkably well and did not have to be convinced of the desirability of laissez faire capitalism as practiced in their contemporary western world (that is, a variety of capitalism that incorporated government intervention, especially in the form of protective tariffs). This was a dominant and triumphant active citizenry, afraid of neither capitalism nor foreigners. But the masses of society, the great majority of the population, needed greater direction and the benefits of a planned economy. It was a very happy situation for the active citizenry until the middle of the nineteenth century when radicals began speaking of democracy or socialism. Until then just about everywhere there had been either an economic surplus or enough of an illusion of it, as David Potter might say, to provide the system with the optimism necessary for capitalism and liberalism to function together relatively smoothly. After 1848 there was an abrupt and rude change in the rules. The optimism was fast dissipating, something most members of the active citizenry could not comprehend. It took until well into the twentieth century for sufficient radicalization of the masses to produce socialist change on a significant scale, but even before the end of the nineteenth century it should have been clear that the earlier brand of capitalism was no longer suited to the needs and desires of the times.

Structurally the economies of the new countries were seriously deficient for their long-term requirements as they struck out on their own in world capitalism. As seen in the discussion of the colonial period there was no proletariat of which to speak. Spanish America was capitalist but with glaring neofeudal holdovers. Too many members of the lower classes were tied to the land by neofeudal arrangements—such as the use of land paid for by a service tenement—for a modern proletariat of significant size to develop. Such a large proletariat would have been either an agrarian or an industrial proletariat. An agrarian proletariat probably would have been radicalized to the point of producing revolution in the rural regions or would have been forced off the land and into the cities, where it would have had to be absorbed by an industrial complex, or it would have been subject to radicalization and revolution. Perhaps an intense proletarianization of the working classes would have forced the active citizenry to protect local industry enough to see it firmly established. The proletariat then would have provided the basis of a market for cheap, coarse manufactures, the stuff of early industrialization. Had there been this industrialization the emergent economies would have been better suited to perform in the world capitalist system.

The independent economies were also structurally unsound in that they lacked a mature craft guild development. The European artisan guilds contributed to the presence of a high standard of business ethic and to the establishment of certain private business institutions that aided the industrial process. It is to be presumed that they would have done so in Spanish America also.

Thus, following Marx's definition of capitalism, we see certain internal factors retarding the Spanish American transition from neofeudal capitalism to industrial capitalism. That Spanish America was ill prepared to compete in the world capitalist market was not the fault of capitalism but of the kind of capitalism that had been practiced in the colonial epoch and that often continued to be practiced during the national period. No major region of Spanish America was flooded by European goods to a significantly greater degree after independence than during the final decades of the colonial period. There is no reason why the new nations could not have protected their economies, especially the few industries they possessed; and, in fact, some nations did. Again, this was not a matter of capitalism or socialism. But how was one to secure recognition from Britain or the United States while keeping out British and North American goods and merchants? It was certainly a ticklish situation, one that was compounded by the fact that many sectors of the active citizenry required a fairly open trading system for economic success. They very much needed foreign markets for the goods they either produced or traded. And often they also ardently desired European industrial products. What is more, they were classically liberal by predisposition and quite naturally capitalists.

Yet for all their enthusiasm—and indeed it was great at times—the new national leaders did not fully appreciate that their countries were becoming neocolonies in the world capitalist system, that values, priorities, and prices were often being determined in foreign metropolises. They did not realize it in part because they liked the system and in part because their economies were generally thriving. The active citizenry, at least, was in very good shape.

Foreign Domination and Foreign Exploitation

No aspect of independent life in Spanish America seems to arouse Spanish Americans and students interested in the area quite so much as the issue of foreign domination and exploitation. Clearly it was one of the gravest problems faced by the new countries. Both the United States and Great Britain saw Spanish America, and Brazil too, as an infinite and enticing new market. No bones were made about this. There was a rivalry between the two powers; they even fought each other in Spanish American waters during the War of 1812. However, there was not so much of a rivalry between the merchants who settled in the new countries. The British merchants had an initial advantage. Great Britain was more advanced industrially, its merchants had greater facilities to offer the Spanish Americans, and it enjoyed special trading privileges with Brazil which permitted it advantages in trading with the rest of the continent. But both countries had great leverage in that the Spanish Americans needed and welcomed foreign merchants and their capital. More than one Spanish American statesman suggested that his country grant one of the major foreign powers a long-term exclusive trading privilege in return for recognition and support. More than one proposed the ceding of national territory to a foreign power as a trading factory in return for recognition and support. One would expect such an atmosphere to be highly attractive to foreign merchants.

And indeed they flocked in. It is said that when news reached Great Britain of the conquest of Buenos Aires by Popham, about a hundred ships were fitted out for trade with the Plate region. When the British took Montevideo in 1807 six thousand British citizens are supposed to have entered the city. Naturally, many were merchants. And merchants from Great Britain, the United States, and other countries set up shop in all the new nations, finding more success in some places than in others. They not only lodged themselves in the leading ports but often in the hinterland also. They quickly became a powerful force, not only economically but politically. The new nations depended on them for arms and ammunition, for capital and credit. And they wanted recognition from the mother countries.

This situation allowed the foreign merchants to exert a good deal of political pressure, especially when British merchants could call on the commander of the British naval forces stationed in nearby waters to support their positions. The precise nature of the political relationship between the new nations and the foreign merchants has not been examined carefully. A recent study of the Chilean relationship with the British between 1817 and 1823 suggests that the British merchants were not as politically powerful as one might suspect. The Chileans acquitted themselves quite well in their political dealings with the foreign merchant community. And when one speaks of resident foreign merchants it usually goes unnoticed that many of them became Spanish American citizens, married Spanish Americans, and sired Spanish American families. We often hear of the great foreign merchant and banking houses at midnineteenth century, but what we do not hear is that many of them were, in any meaningful sense, Spanish American and not foreign. But taking Spanish America as a whole it is certain that the foreign merchants exerted more political influence than many twentieth century nationalists would have liked.

Recognizing that there indeed was economic exploitation by foreigners—that many foreign merchants arrived in Spanish America, stayed a short while, made fortunes (sometimes spectacular ones), and then departed for home—it would still be salutary to see the other side of the picture, to learn something of the contribution of the foreign merchants and foreign capital.

The case of a young Scotsman, John Parish Robertson, is particularly interesting. Robertson traveled to the Plate region first in 1807 and then again the following year. For about two years he worked as a clerk in Buenos Aires. At the end of 1811 he traveled upriver over a thousand miles to Asunción, the capital of Paraguay, where he awaited the arrival of a shipment of goods he was supposed to sell. He was the first British subject to trade directly in the new country. Robertson was successful, and he remained in Asunción for three years. To estimate his financial position, one need note only that some products purchasable at Buenos Aires sold at Asunción ten or twenty times higher. He did so well that in 1814 he had his younger brother, William, come over to join him in the business. But from that point things went bad. Returning from a trip to Buenos Aires he was robbed and nearly killed. Worse, perhaps, he was no longer in favor with the Paraguayan dictator, Francia, and he was expelled from Asunción. He and his brother then established themselves in the provincial town of Corrientes, in the Argentine province of the same name. The province of Corrientes had been one of Argentina's great cattle-producing regions during the colonial period, but the civil wars between the provinces and Buenos Aires that attended the independence movement had seriously disrupted the pastoral economy of Corrientes and its neighboring cattle province of Entre Ríos. Dried hides could be purchased in Corrientes very cheaply and sold in Buenos Aires at an enormous profit and then again in England for another great profit.

The cattle provinces needed two things especially in order to get back on their feet: an effective marketing system for cattle hides and an inducement to put the cattle estates back into shape. Actually, the first would provide the second. The Robertsons supplied the first; they established an efficient and profitable marketing system for the region's hides. And the cattle producers got their estates in order and supplied the hides. Through a partnership with another Scot at Buenos Aires the Robertsons were able to provide credit to the cattle owners and thus allow them to set their estates in order. In a short while both the province of Corrientes and the Robertsons were prospering. Early in 1817 John Parish Robertson returned to England and established a merchant house in Liverpool. William set up shop in Buenos Aires.

What is one to make of the Robertsons? They were two young foreigners who in a matter of a couple of years not only contributed significantly to the economic restoration of the province of Corrientes but made a tidy sum in the process. And in so doing they were not always well appreciated by local Argentine merchants. In both Paraguay and Argentina the two Robertsons supplied a valuable service that local merchants were either unwilling or unable to supply. They helped the economic development of Paraguay and Argentina and in the latter instance made fortunes themselves.

But not all foreigners were quite so lucky. Some, like John Miers, invested small fortunes and lost them, in part due to a Latin approach to business to which their ventures would not adapt. Miers had brought five Englishmen and forty thousand dollars in machinery with him to Chile for the refining of copper and its manufacture into sheets for the American market and the East Indian trade. According to his own account, he had invested another equal amount in the venture once in Chile. After incessant problems with provincial officials, including a lawsuit that dragged on for three years, and then an earthquake, Miers gave up the whole project and migrated to Argentina. Here is one Englishman who did not fare so well in Chile.

William Wheelwright was one of the most famous of the foreigners to work in Spanish America in the decades after independence. Born in Newburyport, Massachusetts, in 1798, to a family of established, wealthy merchants, he acquired a small fortune working as a merchant in Guayaquil, Ecuador, during the late 1820s. In 1829 he settled in Valparaíso, Chile. During the next decades he introduced steam navigation to Pacific South America, built Chile's first railroad, and provided several other important internal improvements. By 1860 he had shifted his attention to Argentina. His Chilean experience is highly instructive for an attempt to understand this phenomenon called foreign exploitation.

Funds for the establishment of the Pacific Steam Navigation Company (the PSNC), which still operates today, had to be raised abroad—in this case in Great Britain—for two fundamental reasons. One is that the Chilean government still functioned under the mercantilist concept of a balanced budget and did not have the money to finance such a company. The other is that the financial energies of the private citizenry were turned elsewhere—to more profitable ventures!

We can learn something about British financial adventurousness and neocolonialism in general from the early life of the PSNC. In December 1844, at the company's second annual shareholders' meeting, the directors announced a loss of over £72,010 during the first four years of operation, on a paid-up capital of £93,905. But from that moment things began to change. Although a breakdown of the steamer *Peru* during 1845 cost the company about 15,000 pesos and a lost coal freighter another 8,000 pesos, the new year saw the company develop a refreshing momentum, stimulated by a mail contract finally arranged with the British government. The contract provided for a regular mail service between Valparaíso and Panama, touching at many intermediary ports. A British government subsidy was fixed at £20,000 per year for five years. The British government was not concerned with any mail contract that the company might have with the Chilean government but only with the service its own contract guaranteed. The company was supposed to use the steamers *Chile* and *Peru*, but the contract induced the directors to order their first iron vessel. Later in the year the iron steamer *Ecuador* was launched.

The new mail contract put Wheelwright as well as the company in a highly optimistic mood. The company's stock had fallen to below £9 from a high of £40, and in 1845 its capital was valued at less than £8,000. It was then that the mail contract was secured. Wheelwright later noted: "Without this contract the Company would not be in existence. The British government resolved to pay this sum because it understood the great public utility of the enterprise and saw that without this aid it would find it impossible to continue forward."[1] Wheelwright wrote this in 1849 at a time when he was attempting to secure the rights for a Santiago-Valparaíso railroad and demonstrate the positive aspects of direct governmental financial aid to the internal improvements industry. And one should bear in mind that given the circumstances there would not likely have been steam navigation in the Pacific during the 1840s were it not for British private capital and public subsidy. It is quite clear that the PSNC was not one of those legendary British colonialist companies that marched into Spanish America, used and abused its hospitality, made a quick and substantial profit, and sent the returns home. It was quite the opposite. In fact, it was not until 1848 that the company really began to get on its feet. The shareholders were rewarded with their first dividend–2.5 percent!

There is an interesting sidelight to the PSNC venture. The company had originally been granted a ten-year exclusive privilege for steam navigation in Chilean coastal waters. The privilege expired in 1850, and Wheelwright made strenuous efforts to secure an extension. One of the country's leading newspapers, the *Progreso* of Santiago, captured the mood of many Chileans. The great benefit the present company could give the country, it suggested, had been given already: "to acclimatize steam in the Pacific . . . this benefit has been paid for by 10 years of monopoly, and of tyranny, to which we resigned ourselves hoping things would become better. The true benefits of steam will come when the privilege has terminated." The newspaper was not intimidated by a merchant fear that the line of steam communication with Europe would be interrupted because "the present line of steamers can do no less than continue and will continue to function, and the apprehension of its disappearance does not merit the immense sacrifice that one must make."[2] In the same edition, it carried a copy of a Peruvian decree which shortly before had ended the PSNC's exclusive privilege for that country.

The exclusive privilege was in fact terminated. Wheelwright's company was now in an awkward position. Its exclusive monopoly had been ended, and it had not sought a needed subvention; but it was forced to continue its operations at an accelerated pace. Lacking both a subvention and a monopoly, the company now had to provide the most frequent and efficient service in its history to date. Rather than allow its equipment to lay idle the company chose to meet the new open competition in a manner Wheelwright had always advocated—better service. Those who feared that loss of the company's exclusive privilege would preclude adequate steam navigation were shortly shown to be incorrect, while others, buoyed up by the confidence which attended the California gold discovery, and favoring cessation of the monopoly, were proved correct.

Another of Wheelwright's ventures is pertinent to our discussion of neocolonialism. He had become interested in railroads even before the PSNC was established. No one had to be convinced of the need for an improved internal communications system; the problem was that the burden of achieving an improved system was considered to belong to the empresario, not to the government. And during the decade of the 1830s—only a few years before the sophisticated demands of nineteenth century technology would make prodigious sums of money necessary for internal improvements—capital was not forthcoming even for the more prosaic forms of internal improvements. In 1833 the important paper the *Mercurio* of Valparaíso noted that capitalists were not eager to invest in low-interest-yielding roads and canals when they could earn in the neighborhood of 18 percent from personal loans and business investments.

This is an extremely important point. It is popular to believe that Chile and the rest of Spanish America lacked capital for their own internal development because it was constantly being expropriated by the world capitalist metropolis. Actually, Chileans and most other Spanish Americans had the capital to finance any of the nineteenth century internal improvements themselves. The reason they had to rely on foreign capital, and the traditional expropriation that goes with it, is that the national capitalists preferred to invest their money in more appealing enterprises, because the governments were not at first willing to take a strong financial part in such ventures and because the new nations did not have a tax structure and collection technique suitable to the new century. In 1835 Chilean Minister of Treasury Manuel Rengifo lamented that if the agricultural sector would pay the government only 10 percent of the value it produced, the government would have enough money to meet all public expenditures. He was talking about the receipt of millions of pesos rather than hundreds of thousands. It was not national or world capitalism but the brand of capitalism practiced in Spanish America that caused the government to lack adequate resources.

Millions of pesos were required for the rail line between Santiago and Valparaíso. It was quite generally acknowledged that the line might not produce even a 5 percent profit on invested capital. There is little wonder that Chilean capitalists would not invest in it when they could get two, three, or four times that return on more traditional and secure investments.

Yet they finally did invest in the Santiago-Valparaíso railroad. Before a contract was granted by the government, Wheelwright, working with domestic capital, had organized and built Chile's first railroad, running from the rich mining region of Copiapó to the port of Caldera in the Atacama desert. In February 1852 the government announced the formation of a company to build a railroad between Santiago and Valparaíso and called for subscriptions. Wheelwright, who had been the great promoter of the line, submitted a plan that would permit him to construct the railroad. The government was interested and immediately appointed a commission to report on the new plan.

In March the president made a trip to Valparaíso, where conferences resulting in the formation of a new company were held. The company was to be capitalized at seven million pesos (a peso was generally equal to a U.S. dollar then), with the government subscribing two million pesos, the gentlemen with whom the president had conferred in Valparaíso contributing another two million pesos, and with three million pesos being reserved for the open market.

William Wheelwright was not included in the negotiations or in the formation of the company. The government was now assuming an active and direct role in the development of internal improvements. The entire financial structure of the railroad was designed to be organized with Chilean capital. The situation had altered markedly since Wheelwright's early days in Chile and the formation of the PSNC.

It appears that Wheelwright was maneuvered out of his contract with the government by a small group of very affluent and confident Chileans. Among them were Matías Cousiño, Angel Custodio Gallo, and Joshua Waddington, who are said to have subscribed two million pesos worth of stock. Cousiño and Gallo had made their fortunes in the northern mining industry; and Waddington, an Englishman-turned-Chilean who was appointed minister of treasury in 1851, had made his in Valparaíso commerce.

From this picture one does not get the impression of foreign imperialism or neocolonialism. The commanding wealth and confidence on the part of Chileans and other Spanish Americans at midnineteenth century suggests why the capitalist classes throughout Spanish America were so receptive to classical economics—to laissez faire capitalism, as modified by the need of governmental intervention in financing internal improvements and protecting industry and agriculture—and were not intimidated by the presence of foreigners in their economies.

There was indeed neocolonialism, and it embarrassed the integrity of the new nations in the decades after independence. Many times foreigners and foreign nations took advantage of the economic and political vulnerability of the emergent states. How demeaning it was for a new government to be presented with a petition signed by a foreign merchant community and supported by the commander of the British naval forces in the region arguing against a tax or for permission to bury Protestant dead. How better balanced and more integrated would have been the new economies had they been subjected to national planning and not the vagaries of capitalism. But after all this was, in fact, the age of capitalism and not socialism, the age of the world capitalist market and not world socialism. Considering that the Spanish American countries really had no other choice but to be capitalist after 1810, they should be given credit for faring quite well in a system that was not always generous to unbalanced and nonindustrial economies. And it was not only neocolonialism that troubled the new nations; there were other problems equally distressing and disturbing.

General Administrative Problems

Some of the problems that challenged the ingenuity of even the most proficient government leaders during the early decades of the nineteenth century are well known and need only be mentioned briefly. Geography and poor transportation facilities worked against national unity and economic growth. It was sometimes cheaper to import agricultural and pastoral products by sea (a notably cheap form of transportation) than to move them domestically even short distances. Some local regions had more contact with the outside world than with valley cultures only ten or twenty miles away. During the decade of the 1820s it sometimes took as much as a year for a United States minister to have his messages from Santiago, Chile, reach Washington. So little confidence did officials place in the shipping facilities that they made a practice of sending several copies of a dispatch, each by a different vessel. In 1836 a sailing ship set a new record of eighty-seven days for the voyage between New York and Valparaíso. It was not until 1845 that a daily mail service was instituted between Santiago and Valparaíso, a distance of eighty-four miles, taking about thirteen and a half hours in each direction. A letter sent from Santiago took nine days to Concepción and about an equal time to Copiapó. And so far as the rest of Spanish America goes, it should be noted that Chile was not retarded in these matters. In Central America the capital of Costa Rica was a thousand miles from Guatemala City. When conditions were good it took at least a month and a half to travel the distance and deliver a message. During the rainy season, which ran nearly half the year, travel between the two capitals was almost impossible. And it was even more difficult for the Central American capitals to communicate with Mexico City.

There were also fundamental social problems. Some of the new countries had large Indian populations. While all the research is not in yet, one may note that for whatever the reasons, Indians did not generally participate in the Western-style economies as readily and effectively as did Europeans, creoles, and even mixed-bloods. And, in fact, early nineteenth century liberalism at times brought about a dismantling of legislation that had protected the Indian during the colonial epoch. One result of independence was that the Indian was thrust boldly into world capitalism without proper preparation or traditional protection. The new situation was not always better than the old. There were even significant numbers of mixed-bloods and people of largely European blood who did not, for one reason or another, participate as actively and effectively in the new economies as they might have done. Those countries in which large segments of whites, reds, blacks, or mixed-bloods chose not to (or were not able to) function well in capitalism saw their economies suffer.

There was also the matter of praetorianism, the militarism that triumphantly carried out the independence movement and not unnaturally wanted a piece of the later action. The crown had started the whole thing by expanding the creole militia and creating the creole army units with creole officers at the end of the colonial period. These soldiers too were entitled to the coveted *fuero*, the right of special jurisdiction in military matters and often civilian affairs. Officers, soldiers, and even their families could be tried in military courts.

Not only did military men often want to govern the new states but they desired a very ample and encompassing *fuero*. The liberal constitutions of the period generally attempted to establish civilian authority over the military. They did so in part by establishing civil militia forces as a counterpoise to the professional military establishment, thereby curtailing the *fuero*. Where the new governments were not successful there often were coups and military intervention. The military tradition established at the end of the colonial period, nurtured and brought to maturity and fulfillment during the wars of independence, seriously undermined the growth and development of many Spanish American nations.

Every nation had its *caudillo* problem. *Caudillos* were the local chieftains, the men whose charisma and physical prowess established them as the leaders of provincial bands and sometimes national populations. At the local level they often disrupted economies and even political structures. Usually they were not military men, since military professionalism was not consonant with the irregularities and freedoms of *caudillismo*. But the line between some *caudillos* and some military officers was decidedly thin. When *caudillos* became national leaders they sometimes provided just the proper ingredient for general growth and development; at other times they had precisely the opposite effect. But much the same could be said about the non-*caudillo* types also.

One of the constantly mentioned problems facing the new nations was the general lack of qualified governmental personnel. All the colonies possessed trained and effective administrative bureaucracies, and these made for an easy transition from colonialism to national government. But the nature of early national government caused a shortage of qualified personnel in many places. All the new nations had congresses, and many had provincial assemblies. These conspicuous republican bodies won the interest and attention of scores of talented men who, although they naturally had no experience at organizing and running legislative bodies and often blundered a bit, in colonial times might have gone into the administrative bureaucracy and done a creditable job. Also, because creoles were restricted from certain high administrative posts in the colonial bureaucracy they seem to have craved the remaining ones quite avidly. This was part of the creole-peninsular controversy. But once independence was achieved it appears that some nationals who ordinarily might have gone into the bureaucracy now found it less appealing. There was nothing to prove, and national recognition and prestige could be achieved elsewhere. Some countries, like Chile, suffered very little from the lack of qualified personnel during the early national period; others, like New Granada, suffered noticeably. But this topic has not actually been studied carefully, and further investigations on the relationship between the bureaucracy and early national problems are needed.

It is often said that the new countries lacked political experience, sometimes even that they were not sufficiently prepared for independence. The new countries did not lack administrative experience; they did, however, lack legislative experience. The two should not be confused. There is a world of difference between running a government and running a legislature. And even so, it took a short time indeed for the Spanish Americans to get the feel of legislative assemblies. The fact that some Spanish Americans did not pay as much attention to the niceties of democratic government as democrats and even some classical liberals would have liked does not mean they lacked political experience; in some instances one might argue that this demonstrated their considerable political maturity. And it is the central point of this chapter that there are no simple answers to why one country developed a stultifying stability and another a disrupting instability, why one witnessed an era of general progress and another an era of retardation. The answers are highly complex.

Finally, there was the church-state problem. In some countries, like Chile, where the church did not become very wealthy and did not own too much land, the issue of religion was decided without a great deal of disruption. In Chile, for instance, the major church properties during the colonial period belonged to the Jesuits, and these were sold at public auction after the Jesuits were expelled in 1767. During the first decades after independence the Chileans did not have to face the power of an overly wealthy church establishment; nor did they need church land. In Mexico the situation was reversed. There the church was excessively wealthy and powerful. A good many people had their eyes on church lands and money. In order for the reformers of the 1830s and thereafter to establish civilian control over the church, to curb church abuses, and to have lay education, they had to be willing to fight and to face the consequences (often insurmountable) of an antagonistic church. In more than one country the alienation of the church brought down governments. In these countries the church issue was one of the most troublesome of all.

Centralism and Federalism

No problem was more ruinous to many of the early national governments than the issue of centralism versus federalism. Federalism had both political and economic origins. In some nations, like Chile, it was more political than economic; in others, like Argentina and Mexico, it was more economic than political, although there were strong and distinct political overtones also. In some places, like Mexico, federalists had (or developed) definite liberal tendencies; in others, like Bogotá, New Granada, the federalists seemed to be more on the conservative side. The examples of two regions will provide further insight into the complicated problems faced by the new national governments.

Central America

The first example is that of Central America. By the end of the colonial period there was wholesale provincial discontent over the power and influence exerted by the capital of the captaincy general, Guatemala City. The growing European textile industry during the eighteenth century made the indigo produced in the captaincy general a highly prized commodity. It was produced primarily in El Salvador and Guatemala and was sent through Guatemala City, where trade in the commodity could be controlled and taxes collected, to a gulf port. The dominant position of Guatemala City and her merchants in this trade was both natural and political. Other provinces benefited by the indigo trade also. While Guatemala and El Salvador produced indigo, Nicaragua and Honduras produced the agricultural and pastoral products needed by the indigo workers. The Central Americans had worked out their own preindustrial balanced economy. The problem was that the Guatemala City merchants controlled the entire process through the advantage of being in the capital city, through purchase power and credit power, and through the power accrued from the distribution of European goods.

During the second half of the eighteenth century provincial producers and merchants became highly dissatisfied with the system and petitioned the crown for reforms. The crown was impressed with the provincial position and took steps to end the monopoly of the Guatemala City merchants. New routes to the coast were to be established, and credit facilities were to be expanded so that provincial growers of indigo would not be so dependent on the Guatemala City merchants. But the reforms were widely circumvented during the final decades of the colonial period, and provincial discontent was not abated. This was basically the economic source of Central American federalism.

There were also political roots of federalism in Central America. Provincial capitals were displeased with the political power exerted by Guatemala City. But even at the provincial level there was a conflict among cities for political ascendancy, or at least relative autonomy. Between 1808 and the declaration of complete independence from

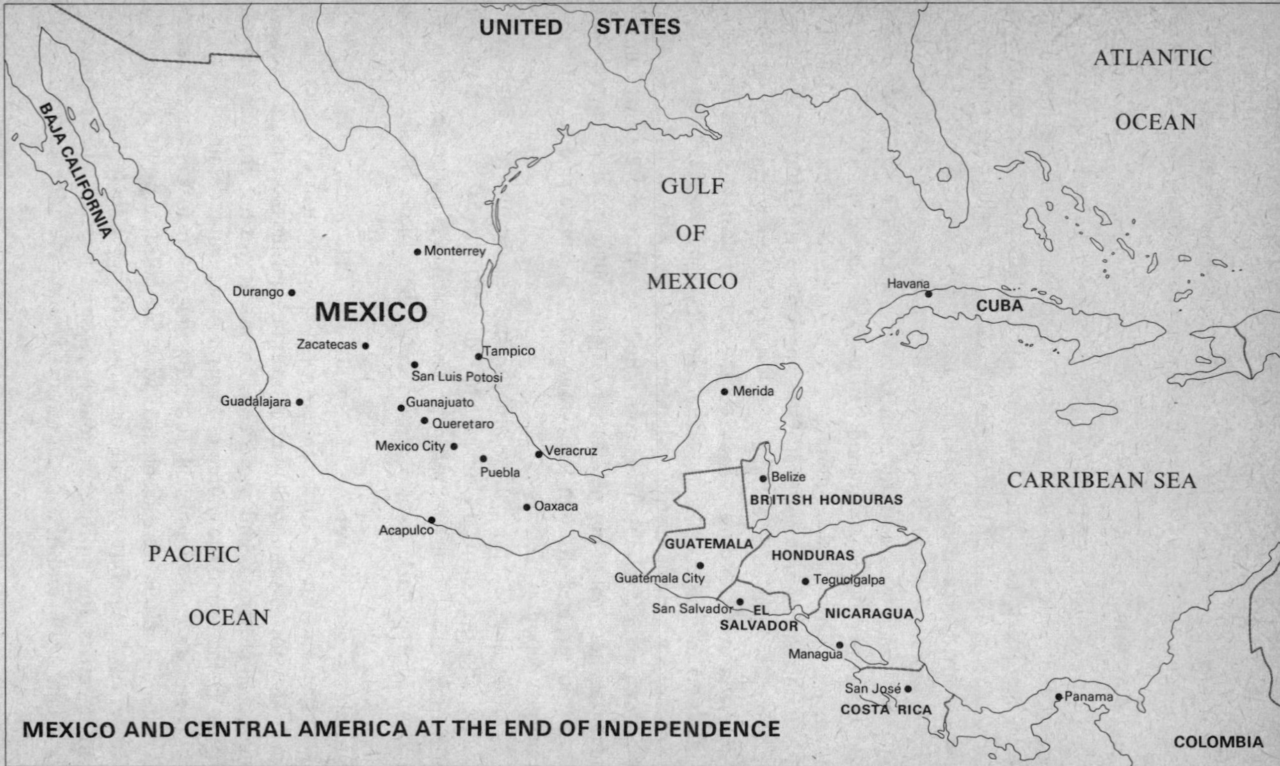

MEXICO AND CENTRAL AMERICA AT THE END OF INDEPENDENCE

foreign powers, including Mexico, in 1823, there were many local revolts, some of which pitted one provincial town against another. When Central America joined Iturbide's Mexican empire in 1822 it did so mainly because some of the provinces preferred to be under the political tutelage of distant Mexico City rather than Guatemala City. With Iturbide's fall from power in 1823 the Central American states declared their independence and drafted the constitution of 1824. The new organic code established the federal republic of Central America.

What the Central Americans had done was to recreate the old captaincy general of Guatemala, without the province of Chiapas (which remained a part of Mexico), in such a way as to enjoy the benefits of unity and at the same time not suffer the dominance of the former province of Guatemala. Thus a new nation was created where it was needed. The economy of the new republic had great potential. The first congress met in 1825, but in 1826 there was already a major civil war, which lasted three years. There was further warfare for another two years. By 1831 the economy of the republic was in sad shape, and its political structure was less than sound.

By the end of the decade the federal republic of Central America (which by then was really more of a confederation than a federal republic) ceased to exist, and a series of Central American nations took its place. No part of Spanish America needed national unity and some form of federated central government and unified economy more than Central America. The failure of the former captaincy general to achieve its uncommon potential was not due to any one reason, certainly not merely to neocolonialism.

Argentina

The second example is that of Argentina. The provinces of the former viceroyalty of the Río de la Plata had almost as difficult a time coming together as did those of Guatemala. It took them until past the middle of the nineteenth century to do so. One might say the issue was not finally settled until 1880, when the city of Buenos Aires became a federalized district. But by the 1860s Argentina was functioning as one political and economic unit, although the province of the Banda Oriental was by then long independent as the republic of Uruguay.

No country that became united and remained so had a more difficult time doing it than Argentina. And for decades it often looked as though the city and province of Buenos Aires would not be able to bring the other provinces into any sort of unified state. The issue of federalism or centralism nearly Balkanized Argentina; the great economic entity of Argentina almost did not reach fulfillment.

The problem in Argentina was particularly economic. Leaving aside the Banda Oriental, the former viceroyalty was divided into two distinct economic regions. First and foremost was the city and province of Buenos Aires. The city of Buenos Aires was the capital of the viceroyalty, and it controlled the customs revenues for the entire region. The city and port of Buenos Aires was the commercial entrepôt for the entire former viceroyalty. It consumed goods produced by the other provinces, although it was not dependent on them since its needs could be supplied easily and often more cheaply from abroad. The city's merchants brought in and distributed European goods. The province as a whole thrived on foreign trade.

The rest of the former viceroyalty was made up of the interior provinces, including Córdoba, Tucumán, Santiago del Estero, San Juan, and Mendoza; and the littoral provinces of Corrientes, Santa Fe, and Entre Ríos. The interior provinces produced a whole range of goods, including hides, textiles, cotton, and fruits from Córdoba; wines and dried fruits from Mendoza; and hides, leather, cotton, timber, cheese, dried fruits, wines, and many other items from Tucumán and San Juan. These products were shipped to Buenos Aires, where they were consumed or transshipped to other provinces and abroad. In turn Buenos Aires sent back products produced in its province and abroad.

There was a genuine conflict of interest here. Buenos Aires needed relatively free trade. It wanted to sell the pastoral products produced in its province and import foreign goods. Its pastoral products sold well abroad and did not have to be protected against foreign pastoral products. Nor did Buenos Aires want to protect local industry—of which the province had little—at the risk of restricting the influx of foreign commodities, the source of its economic prosperity. On the other hand the interior provinces sorely needed protection, not only for their local industries, which could not compete with the cheaper foreign goods, but also for some of their agricultural products, most especially wine, which also could not withstand foreign competition.

The relationship of Buenos Aires and the littoral provinces was fundamentally one of conflict. The riparian provinces produced essen-

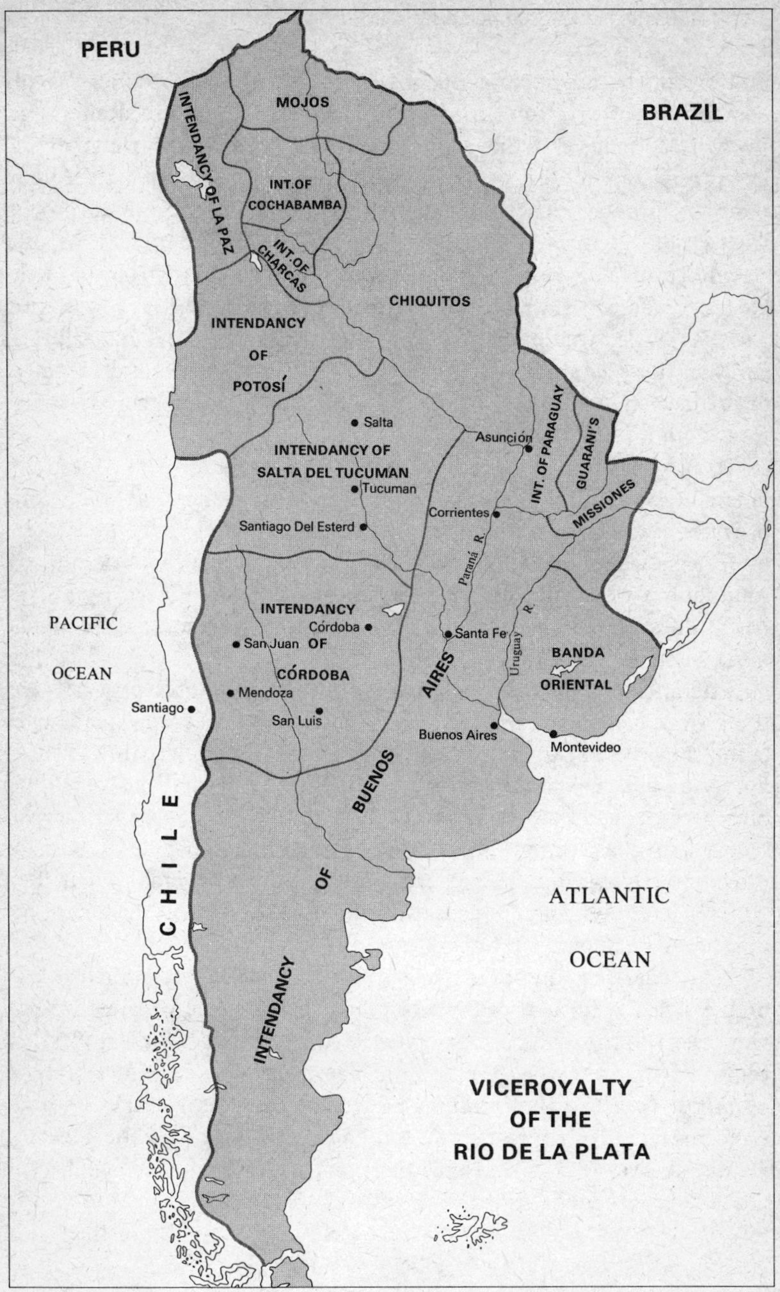

PERU
BRAZIL
MOJOS
INTENDANCY OF LA PAZ
INT.OF COCHABAMBA
INT.OF CHARCAS
CHIQUITOS
INTENDANCY OF POTOSÍ
Salta
INTENDANCY OF SALTA DEL TUCUMAN
Tucuman
Santiago Del Esterd
Asunción
INT. OF PARAGUAY
GUARANI'S
MISSIONES
Corrientes
Paraná R.
INTENDANCY OF CÓRDOBA
Córdoba
San Juan
Mendoza
San Luis
Santa Fe
Uruguay R.
BANDA ORIENTAL
Buenos Aires
Montevideo
PACIFIC OCEAN
Santiago
CHILE
INTENDANCY OF BUENOS AIRES
ATLANTIC OCEAN
VICEROYALTY OF THE RIO DE LA PLATA

tially what the province of Buenos Aires did—pastoral products, highly competitive on the foreign market. These provinces also desired relatively free trade; and they opposed protection for industries they did not possess, at the risk of seeing tariffs raised abroad against the items they did produce. Their conflict with Buenos Aires centered around who should control the foreign trade and customs duties to its own advantage. The port of Buenos Aires controlled the entrance to the Paraná River, along which lay the provinces of Corrientes, Entre Ríos, and Santa Fe. Oceangoing vessels could travel up the Paraná just as easily as they could stop at Buenos Aires. Thus the littoral provinces could have traded directly with Europe and collected their own customs duties.

To protect their interests the interior and littoral provinces desired a federal system. The interior provinces wanted protection; the littoral provinces wanted to replace the port of Buenos Aires as the focal point of foreign trade, or at least to win a more equitable share of the customs duties (the chief source of public revenues) produced by it. The battle lines were drawn; it took half a century to resolve these fundamental issues.

Attempts to arrive at a working solution of the problems between the province of Buenos Aires and the other provinces were made even before independence was officially declared in 1816, but they were to no avail. The centralist constitution of 1819 naturally favored the province of Buenos Aires and was repudiated by the other provinces. A succeeding constitution of 1826 had little better luck in uniting the provinces. During the next decades the provinces generally went their own ways, united among themselves sometimes formally and sometimes informally in a confederation.

The federalist question frustrated both political and economic progress in the former viceroyalty. Even the province of Buenos Aires witnessed political disruption over its own version of the federalist-centralist controversy. Other provinces often were run by local *caudillos*. None of the interior or littoral provinces had an easy time achieving economic prosperity. The main source of public revenues almost always was the customs duty, and the amount collected often did not meet public expenditures. Yet the provinces did not desire independence for themselves. They well understood that their best interests lay in a mutually cooperative, united, and federalist country that treated their local economic and political interests fairly.

It is quite clear that Argentina would have done much better both economically and politically had all the provinces been able to arrive at an efficacious solution to their federalist-centralist problems during the early years after independence.

The Practical Problems of Daily Government

No picture of the many disturbing and debilitating problems faced by the early national governments would be complete without inclusion of at least some of the more ordinary, mundane problems of everyday government. These often were more disruptive to the growth and development of independent Spanish America than the more complex problems of neocolonialism and federalism.

In almost every instance public revenues could not meet public expenditures. This was due to several reasons. The most important was the war of independence itself. The many new governments–like Argentina, Chile, Peru, Gran Colombia–that prosecuted the war even after their own independence was more or less secure were strapped with an enormous financial problem. In some places the war disrupted the economy, which made for less public revenue. To pay for the war the new governments had to resort to forced loans and expropriation of royalist property. They also went into debt, taking on foreign loans for which they had to pay premium interest rates. These loans themselves became a further burden on national treasuries. Most problematic of all perhaps was that the new governments often could not pay the military properly, or even what little they were supposed to pay it. The poor salaries, added to the effort of the early national governments to establish civilian authority over the military, often alienated a powerful interest group that at times overthrew governments.

When speaking of finances and qualified personnel one should recall that the early national governments had to support two costly institutions not known to the colonial system. Each country had its own congress, often with two branches and provincial counterparts, and its independent judiciary. There were judges in the colonial era, but the system of courts inherent in liberal republicanism was far more imposing and demanding. All the judges and congressmen had to be paid, and this placed an additional strain on the already precarious financial structures. Many more qualified people were required by the national bureaucracies than by their predecessors. It was often difficult to find them, although there were probably more around than is generally supposed. Many men who would have made excellent congressmen, judges, or general administrative bureaucrats preferred other callings. The weak financial structures dictated low salaries, and many men were forced to devote their attention to establishing or recouping their personal fortunes. It was not always easy to leave the provinces for the capital and a low-paying, high-prestige position, while others—nationals and foreigners alike—were at home busy making money.

And having these congresses and judiciaries was both awkward and perplexing. It was not at all clear which laws of the colonial past should apply to the national period. A whole compendium of new legislation had to be interpreted, sometimes leading to procrastination and confusion. And it was not clear how a congress should function. Especially obscure was the appropriate relationship between the senate and president. As noted earlier the senate usually considered itself the special guardian of liberalism, an attitude that often put it in direct conflict with the executive branch. It was not unusual for presidential powers to be curtailed, something that limited executive effectiveness. This at times led to ineffectual central government or to a coup headed by the president or the military.

There were so many awesome problems confronting the newly independent nations of Spanish America that there is little wonder so few of them were even fairly successful at meeting the challenges of independence and the nineteenth century. There was no single cause of the political instability or retrograde stability that often followed independence, or of the unstable and ineffectual economies. It was not neocolonialism alone, or federalism, or the church, or geography, or the lack of political experience that did it. It was an entirely complex situation. Here one problem was paramount, there another, but most often it was a combination of the several problems that contrived to limit the possibilities of progress—of growth and development—in the new nations.

Notes

1. Quoted in Jay Kinsbruner, "The Business Activities of William Wheelwright in Chile, 1829-1860" (unpublished doctoral dissertation, New York University, 1964), p. 113.

2. Quoted in Ibid., p. 128.

CHAPTER SEVEN

Conclusion

It was monumental, often violent and cataclysmic, this independence movement that disrupted one of the world's great empires and gave rise to sixteen independent nations. Major military expeditions were undertaken—distinguished expeditions, but often ones that not surprisingly rendered whole regions senseless. At times the individual could hardly fathom the purpose of it all, could hardly see the reason for the hardship that followed so naturally upon the rhetoric. It was a civil war, not only because the colonies were fighting against the mother country essentially for the privilege of home rule, but also because the war split the colonies themselves into royalists and patriots. It even split families; the famous Spanish American family groups were often shocked at their very foundations. How it must have been for those patriarchs who saw their relatives at each others' throats! It was a civil war, and an ugly one.

It was not a revolution. It was not a war for a radical change of government or a major alteration in social structures. It was carried out by the active citizenry for the active citizenry. The masses fought along with one side or another, at times according to no recognizable pattern. Although they paid for independence with their lives—tens of thousands of them, even hundreds of thousands of them—they benefited very little for their efforts. Surely the active citizenry, steeped in paternalism and imbued with a sense of *noblesse oblige*, thought they were doing a fine thing for the people. Slavery, after all, was almost everywhere abolished, and Indian burdens were lessened. That this was not enough did not seem to matter very much to the active citizenry. To compound the situation the disruption of the crown's paternalistic government often left the Indian less protected than previously.

But it was a particularly fine moment for the active citizenry. This was the oligarchy and the people on the way up, the people who counted. The core, the heart of this citizenry was the urban-based bourgeoisie, including the mineowners and even many agrarians. The active citizenry determined the rationale of government, economics, and society in the new nations. The importance of the bourgeoisie in this active citizenry and its impress on the creation of the new nations is often underrated. The bourgeois belief in contractual government; its firm dedication to Lockean liberalism, the individual, and his rights to private property; its class conception of the open society; its dependence on continuous technological improvement; and its confidence and assertiveness that encouraged it to compete in the world capitalist market and not fear foreigners—these were traits that very much characterized the emergent nations, that gave them many of their strengths and weaknesses.

Finally, why the problems, why the seemingly eternal underdevelopment? After all, the colonial economy had been centrally capitalist all along; there was a dynamic and forceful urban-based bourgeoisie that was quite like its counterparts in the rest of the Western world; and Spanish American intellectualism was both brilliant and abreast of international developments. The answer is highly complicated.

It was precisely because Spanish America had a colonial-capitalist economy that it developed a dependent status in the world market.

This could not be turned around in 1810. Great numbers of people did not participate in the local economies, living essentially at the subsistence level and not contributing to the creation of impressive national markets. The early national governments required arms and ammunition, sometimes capital and expertise. They became dependent on foreigners to do things that their own people, who often had the capital and knowledge, refused to do. And the bourgeois predilection for classical liberalism and liberal economics often made the foreigners welcome guests. Sometimes the problem was neocolonialism; at other times it was the issue of federalism or centralism, geography, a fight with the church, a lack of political experience and qualified personnel, the absence of a good money crop or product that could compete on the international market effectively over great periods of time, the presence in some places of enormous numbers of people who would not or could not function to their own benefit in the world capitalist system, or the presence sometimes of a few powerful oligarchs who were decidedly backward and determined against progress. These problems appeared in various combinations and intensity. Spanish America's continued troubles and underdevelopment have not been due to any one of them alone.

Bibliographical Note

The first section of this selected bibliography comprises works in English and is designed to suggest further readings and to indicate some of the sources used in writing the present book. An attempt was made not to be exhaustive. Many older books familiar to generations of Latin Americanists are not included. Also not included are scores of more recent books and articles that in their own right are valuable but that did not seem to fit the purposes of a selected bibliography. The second section is meant especially for specialists in Latin American history and includes works in Spanish that were particularly important for the development of my own point of view and the writing of this book. As such the bibliography includes some works that were significant to the book in that they led me to positions somewhat different from those intended by the authors. Here also works not immediately important to me were not included. Many contributions well known to specialists—by Restrepo, Alamán, Gianello, Encina, and a host of others—are therefore not included.

I have indicated disagreement with some selections. The nature and extent of this disagreement will be obvious to the reader who compares the present book with those selections.

English Sources

Several books not directly related to the study of Spanish American history were important to the development of the present volume and are recommended to the reader. Guido de Ruggiero, *The History of European Liberalism* (Boston, 1964) is an excellent study of the topic. In addition to the general works of Marx and Lenin, three books were especially important to the present volume: E. J. E. Hobsbawm's introduction to Karl Marx's *Pre-Capitalist Economic Formations* (New York, 1966); Paul M. Sweezy, *The Theory of Capitalist Development* (New York, 1968); and Maurice Dobb, *Studies in the Development of Capitalism*, rev. ed. (New York, 1968). Influential in the development of my thought was Andre Gunder Frank's *Capitalism and Underdevelopment in Latin America* (New York, 1969), with which I disagree considerably. For a conceptual understanding of the colonial system see Max Weber, *The Theory of Social and Economic Organization* (New York, 1969). On feudalism see Marc Bloch, *Feudal Society*, 2 vols. (Chicago, 1966); Henri Pirenne, *Medieval Cities* (Princeton, 1969); and E. J. E. Hobsbawm, "A Case of Neo-Feudalism: La Convención, Peru," *Journal of Latin American Studies*, vol. 1, pt. 2 (November 1969). Two other books were important to me and are highly recommended: E. H. Carr, *The New Society* (New York, 1969) and G. D. H. Cole, *Studies in Class Structure* (London, 1964).

For a general introduction to the colonial period three books will be especially useful to the reader: Bailey W. Diffie, *Latin American Civilization* (Harrisburg, 1945); Charles Gibson, *Spain in America* (New York, 1966); and Clarence H. Haring, *The Spanish Empire in America* (New York, 1963). Many general textbooks provide a worthwhile introduction to the independence period. Very important to me has been John E. Fagg, *Latin America*, rev. ed. (New York, 1969). I have followed Professor Fagg's general discussion for parts of my chapter on the events of independence. For an excellent survey of the historiography of the independence movement see R. A. Humphreys and John Lynch, eds., *The Origins of the Latin American Revolutions, 1808-1826* (New York, 1965). For the role of major foreign powers in the independence movement the student should start with the appropriate selections in the Humphreys and Lynch book.

On Spain see Jaime Vicens Vives's important *An Economic History of Spain* (Princeton, 1969). Very valuable is J. H. Elliot, *Imperial Spain, 1469-1716* (New York, 1966). On the Enlightenment in Spain see Richard Herr, *The Eighteenth-Century Revolution in Spain* (Princeton, 1969). Herr's contribution makes it unnecessary for the general reader to contend with Jean Sarrailh's *La España ilustrada de la segunda mitad del siglo XVIII* (Mexico City, 1957). In addition to Herr see also Robert J. Shafer, *The Economic Societies in the Spanish World, 1763-1821* (Syracuse, 1958).

For both the colonial period and the nineteenth century see Stanley J. and Barbara H. Stein's provocative *The Colonial Heritage of Latin America* (New York, 1970), an essay with which I often disagree. On many topics R. A. Humphreys, *Tradition and Revolt in Latin America* (New York, 1969) is very useful. On the church see John Lloyd Mecham, *Church and State in Latin America*, rev. ed. (Chapel Hill, 1966) and N. M. Farriss, *Crown and Clergy in Colonial Mexico, 1795-1821* (London, 1968). I was especially influenced by Farriss's excellent book. One of the few studies in English on the merchants is D. A. Brading's important *Miners and Merchants in Bourbon Mexico, 1763-1810* (Cambridge, 1971). Also worthwhile is Ralph Lee Woodward, Jr., *Class Privilege and Economic Development: The Consulado de Comercio of Guatemala, 1793-1871* (Chapel Hill, 1966) and Brian R. Hamnett, *Politics and Trade in Southern Mexico, 1750-1821* (Cambridge, 1971). On the workings of the colonial system see John Leddy Phelan's significant *The Kingdom of Quito in the Seventeenth Century: Bureaucratic Politics in the Spanish Empire* (Madison, 1967). Phelan presents a stimulating conceptual discussion, part of which is aimed at Richard M. Morse's "The Heritage of Latin America," a chapter in Louis Hartz, *The Founding of New Societies* (New York, 1964). Morse is one of our most intellectually oriented historians, and here he has presented a major interpretative essay, with which I disagree on several central points. A follow-up on the Morse essay is Magali Sarfatti, *Spanish Bureaucratic-Patrimonialism in America* (Berkeley, 1966). An important study of the colonial machinery is John Lynch, *Spanish Colonial Administration, 1782-1810: The Intendant System in the Viceroyalty of the Río de la Plata* (London, 1958). See also J. R. Fisher, *Government and Society in Colonial Peru: The Intendant System, 1784-1814* (London, 1970), and Leon G. Campbell, "A Colonial Establishment: Creole Domination of the Audiencia of Lima During the Late Eighteenth Century," *Hispanic American Historical Review*, vol. 52, no. 1 (February, 1972). There are several important works on society at the end of the colonial period. Highly recommended is Magnus Mörner, *Race Mixture in the History of Latin America* (Boston, 1967). Of considerable influence has been Lyle N. McAlister, "Social Structure and Social Change in New Spain," *Hispanic American Historical Review*, vol. 43, no. 2 (August, 1963) and his *The "Fuero Militar" in New Spain, 1764-1800* (Gainesville, 1957). See also Marcello Carmagnani, "Colonial Latin American Demography: Growth of Chilean Population, 1700-1830," *Journal of Social History*, vol. 1, no. 2 (Winter, 1967). Two papers done by students of mine were of use to me in writing the present volume: Ricardo Arnaldo's "The Social Structure of Venezuela Prior to Independence" and John G. Bernardino's "Historiography of Mexican Society at the End of the Viceroyalty."

On the causes of independence see Brian R. Hamnett, "The Appropriation of Mexican Church Wealth by the Spanish Bourbon Government–The 'Consolidación de Vales Reales,' " *Journal of Latin American Studies*, vol. 1, pt.2 (November, 1969). For the Enlightenment see Arthur P. Whitaker, ed., *Latin America and the Enlightenment*, 2d. ed. (Ithaca, 1961) and Jefferson Rea Spell, *Rousseau in the Spanish World before 1833* (Austin, 1938).

I have been very influenced by the work of Eduardo Arcila Farías. A selection of his work in English is to be found in the Humphreys and Lynch book. On Túpac Amaru see Lillian Estelle Fisher, *The Last Inca Revolt, 1780-1783* (Norman, Oklahoma, 1966).

On the political thought of the independence movement and early nineteenth century see José Luis Romero, *A History of Argentine Political Thought* (Stanford, 1963); Simon Collier, *Ideas and Politics of Chilean Independence, 1808-1833* (Cambridge, 1967); Charles A. Hale, *Mexican Liberalism in the Age of Mora, 1821-1853* (New Haven, 1968);

and Luis Villoro, "The Ideological Currents of the Epoch of Independence," in Mario de la Cueva, ed., *Major Trends in Mexican Philosophy* (Notre Dame, Indiana, 1966). I have been particularly impressed with Villoro's views on the existence and role of the bourgeoisie in early national Mexican history. For the Cádiz *Cortes* see Nettie Lee Benson, ed., *Mexico and the Spanish Cortes, 1810-1822* (Austin, 1966) and James F. King, "American Representation in the Cortes of Cádiz," *Hispanic American Historical Review*, vol. 33, no. 1 (February, 1953). The special problem of *caudillismo* is treated in Robert L. Gilmore, *Caudillism and Militarism in Venezuela, 1810-1910* (Athens, Ohio, 1964) and Roger M. Haigh, "The Creation and Control of a Caudillo," *Hispanic American Historical Review*, vol. 44, no. 4 (November, 1964). For federalism see Miron Burgin's pioneering *The Economic Aspects of Argentine Federalism, 1820-1852* (Cambridge, Mass., 1946); John Street, *Artigas and the Emancipation of Uruguay* (Cambridge, 1959); and Thomas L. Karnes, *The Failure of Union: Central America, 1824-1960* (Chapel Hill, 1961). For further information on Central America see Mario Rodriguez, *Central America* (Englewood Cliffs, N.J., 1965). A book that covers a myriad of topics, and well, is David Bushnell's *The Santander Regime in Gran Colombia* (Newark, Del., 1954). Charles W. Arnade's *The Republic of Bolivia* (Gainesville, 1957) is interesting on Bolivian developments to independence. For important information on rural society see Arnold J. Bauer's "Chilean Rural Labor in the Nineteenth Century," *The American Historical Review*, vol. 76, no. 4 (October, 1971).

There are innumerable biographies of the liberators. A good place to start is William Spence Robertson's *Rise of the Spanish-American Republic; As Told in the Lives of Their Liberators* (New York, 1961). Two recent paperbacks that deal with Bolívar are worthwhile: John J. Johnson, *Simón Bolívar and Spanish American Independence: 1783-1830* (New York, 1968) and David Bushnell, *The Liberator, Simón Bolívar* (New York, 1970). Both are edited paperbacks. Bushnell has presented a series of documents about Bolívar, and Johnson has presented both documents and a long and interesting introduction. But the standard Bolívar biography in English is Gerhard Masur, *Simón Bolívar*, 2d. ed. (Albuquerque, 1969). For Bolívar's political thought the reader is urged to see Víctor Andrés Belaúnde, *Bolívar and the Political Thought of the Spanish American Revolution* (Baltimore

1938). Two recent studies of Mexican leaders are important: Hugh M. Hamill, Jr., *The Hidalgo Revolt* (Gainesville, 1966) and William H. Timmons, *Morelos: Priest, Soldier, Statesman* (El Paso, 1963).

Finally, since some of my own works played an important part in the preparation of this volume, I thought it appropriate to mention them. The influence of two books on the present volume will be obvious to anyone who reads them. They are *Diego Portales: Interpretative Essays on the Man and Times* (The Hague, 1967) and *Bernardo O'Higgins* (New York, 1968). Much information was taken from my doctoral dissertation, "The Business Activities of William Wheelwright in Chile, 1829-1860" (New York University, 1964), and two articles, "The Political Influence of the British Merchants Resident in Chile during the O'Higgins' Administration, 1817-1823," *The Americas*, vol. 25, no. 1 (July, 1970) and "The Political Status of the Chilean Merchants at Independence: The Concepción Example, 1790-1810," vol. 29, no. 1 (July, 1972). Some of the information concerning the town and province of Concepción in the present volume was taken from documents that I hope will eventually appear as part of a future study.

Spanish Sources

For the colonial period and all other periods Diego Barros Arana's *Historia general de Chile*, 2d. ed., 12 vols. (Santiago, 1930-1941) has always been of great inspiration to me. See also Francisco A. Encina, *Historia de Chile, desde la prehistoria hasta 1891*, 20 vols. (Santiago, 1948-1955) for a series of provocative views. I was drawn to the independence movement in part by reading Julio Alemparte's thoughtful *El Cabildo en Chile colonial*, 2d. ed. (Santiago, 1966). On the workings of the colonial economy see Ruggiero Romano, *Una economía colonial: Chile en el siglo XVIII* (Buenos Aires, 1965) and Marcello Carmagnani's Italian article, "Formazione di un mercato coloniale: Cile, 1680-1830," *Rivista storica italiana* (Anno LXXXI, Fascicolo III). I have not always agreed with Romano or Carmagnani, but I have always been stimulated intellectually by them.

On the causes of independence one must read the Congreso Hispanoamericana de Historia, *Causas y carácteres de la independencia* (Madrid, 1953). Interesting also is the Consejo Superior de Investigaciones Científicas, *Estudios sobre la emancipación de Hispanoamerica* (Madrid,

1963). A great source of articles on the independence movement is *El Movimiento emancipador de Hispanoamerica*, 4 vols. (Caracas, 1961). There is also, naturally, Charles C. Griffin's *Los Temas sociales y económicos en la época de la independencia* (Caracas, 1962). On the colonial economy and the causes of independence Sergio Villalobos's *El Comercio y la crisis colonial* (Santiago, 1968); Hernán Ramírez Necochea's *Antecedentes económicos de la independencia de Chile*, 2d. ed. (Santiago, 1967); and Luis Vitale's *Interpretación marxista de la historia de Chile: La Colonia y la Revolución de 1810* (Santiago, 1969) are all full of information and stimulating thought. (For evidence that contradicts the view of a "colonial siesta" see especially Villalobos.) See also Inge Wolff, "Algunas consideraciones sobre causas económicas de la emancipación chilena," *Anuario de estudios americanos*, vol. II (1954). On the political side of the issue of causes see Villalobos, *Tradición y reforma en 1810* (Santiago, 1961); Jaime Eyzaguirre, *Ideario y ruta de la emancipación chilena* (Santiago, 1957); Lincoln Machado Ribas, *Movimientos revolucionarios* (Montevideo, 1940); and Richard Konetzke, "La Condición legal de los criollos y las causas de la independencia," *Estudios ameracanos*, vol. 1 (January 1950. Enrique de Gandía's *La Independencia Americana* (Buenos Aires, 1961) is fascinating, especially on first reading. On merchants, see Mercedes Alvarez, *Commercio y comerciantes* (Caracas, 1963). For many topics related to this book, including the intellectual origins of independence, see O. Carlos Stoetzer's valuable *El Pensamiento político en la América Española durante el período de la emancipación (1789-1825)*, 2 vols. (Madrid, 1966). On the late colonial revolts see Boleslao Lewin's provocative *La Insurrección de Túpac Amaru*, 2d. ed. (Buenos Aires, 1967) and Daniel Valcarcel, *La Rebelión de Túpac Amaru*, 3rd. ed. (Lima, 1970). See also Pablo E. Cárdenas Acosta *El Movimiento comunal de 1781 en el Nuevo Reino de Granada*, 2 vols. (Bogotá, 1960). Interesting related material may be found in Enrique Florescano, *Precios del maíz y crisis agrícolas en México* (*1708-1810*) (Mexico City, 1969) and Germán Colmenares, *La Provincia de Tunja en el Nuevo Reino de Granada* (Bogotá 1970). See also Marcello Carmagnani's "La Oposición a los tributos," *Revista chilena de historia y geografía*, no. 129 (1961). For one of the few valuable regional studies see Edberto Oscar Acevedo, *La Intendencia de salta del Tucumán en el Virreinato del Río de la Plata* (Mendoza, Argentina, 1965). Acevedo plays down the creole-peninsular controversy. He is duly impressed, properly I think, with the integrated nature of the oligarchy. See also his *Rebelíon de 1767 en el Tucumán* (Mendoza, Argentina, 1969) for a study of an oligarchic uprising.

For the period of independence itself and the early nineteenth century many articles that influenced me are in volumes mentioned above. Of enormous importance to this period are the five volumes published in Caracas in 1961 under the title *El Pensamiento constitucional hispanoamericano hasta 1830* and the five volumes published there the following year under the title *El Pensamiento constitucional de Latinoamerica, 1810-1830*. The volumes contain many significant articles and all the constitutions of the period. On the church see Pedro de Leturia, *Relacciones entre la Santa Sede e Hispanoamerica, 1493-1835*, 3 vols. (Caracas, 1959). An interesting collections of essays on Cádiz is María Isabel Arriazu et al., *Estudios sobre Cortes de Cádiz* (Pamplona, Spain, 1967). An important study of society during the early national period is Catalina Sierra, *El Nascimiento de México* (Mexico City, 1960). For the independence movement in Mexico see Luis Villoro's significant *El Proceso ideológico de la revolución de independencia*, 2d. ed. (Mexico City, 1967). Because of the interests of the author and the range of his coverage, Bartolomé Mitre's *Historia de San Martín* (Buenos Aires, 1950) has always been of use to me. I have invariably found my ventures into Miguel Luis Amunátegui's *Los precursores de la independencia de Chile*, 3 vols. (Santiago, 1910) and his *La Crónica de 1810*, 2 vols. (Santiago, 1876) very rewarding.

Index